FROM
GOTHIC
REVIVAL
TO
FUNCTIONAL
FORM

———————————

DA CAPO PRESS SERIES IN
ARCHITECTURE AND DECORATIVE ART
General Editor: ADOLF K. PLACZEK

Avery Librarian, Columbia University

FROM GOTHIC REVIVAL TO FUNCTIONAL FORM

A STUDY
IN VICTORIAN THEORIES
OF DESIGN

By

ALF BØE

DA CAPO PRESS • NEW YORK • 1979

Library of Congress Cataloging in Publication Data

Bøe, Alf.
   From Gothic revival to functional form.

   (Da Capo Press series in architecture and decora-
tive art)
   Originally presented as the author's thesis,
Oxford, 1954.
   Reprint of the 1st ed. published by Oslo University
Press which was issued as no. 6 of Oslo studies
in English.
   Bibliography: p.
   Includes index.
   1. Design — Great Britain — History — 19th century.
I. Title. II. Series: Norwegian studies in
English; no. 6.
[NK1443.B62   1979]   745.4'49'41   78-31194
ISBN 0-306-77544-1

Published by Da Capo Press, Inc.
A Subsidiary of Plenum Publishing Corporation
227 West 17th Street, New York, N.Y. 10011

FROM
GOTHIC
REVIVAL
TO
FUNCTIONAL
FORM

FROM
GOTHIC
REVIVAL
TO
FUNCTIONAL
FORM

A STUDY
IN VICTORIAN THEORIES
OF DESIGN

By

ALF BØE

OSLO 1957
OSLO UNIVERSITY PRESS

OXFORD: BASIL BLACKWELL

OSLO STUDIES IN ENGLISH, NO. 6

Publications of the British Institute in the University of Oslo

General editors:

Professor Paul Christophersen, Professor Kristian Smidt

———————————————

Printed on a grant from
The Norwegian Research Council for Science
and the Humanities

Printed in Norway
by Hestholms Boktrykkeri

TO MY FATHER

ACKNOWLEDGEMENTS

This book was originally submitted in the spring of 1954 as a thesis for the degree of Bachelor of Letters in the University of Oxford. Since then no very important changes have been made, except in the arrangement of the chapters, and in the introductory and concluding sections which have been entirely recast.

I feel deeply indebted to the authorities of Oslo University, who for two successive years granted me the Norway Scholarship to Wadham College, and I am equally indebted to Wadham College and the University to which it belongs. Without their generous support any thought of carrying on extensive studies in England would have been out of the question.

To a number of private persons I owe very sincere thanks: to Mr. T. S. R. Boase, President of Magdalen College, for his friendly advice particularly in my first year at Oxford. To my teacher and adviser, the late Professor Anders Bugge, of Oslo University, whose all too early death is lamented by students deeply in his debt. To Mr. M. Dodderidge, head of the British Council in Oslo, who read through the final version of the book and suggested some re-phrasings. To the late Mr. Humphry House, Fellow of Wadham College, who with his rare knowledge of 19th century England was an inspiring commentator on my thesis. Mention should also be made of Dr. Thor Kielland, Director of the Oslo Museum of Arts and Crafts; of my friend and fellow student, Mr. Stephan Tschudi Madsen, with whom I have had many stimulating discussions; and of the editors of Oslo Studies in English, who accepted my book for publication. Last, but not least, I am indebted to my wife for her support and help throughout.

To the staff of the Circulation Department of the Victoria and Albert Museum, London, my thanks are also due. Through a happy coincidence their well-documented exhibition of *Victorian and Edwardian Decorative Arts* was opened at the beginning of my stay in England in 1952, and I was generously allowed to study much original material collected for that occasion. Mr. Peter Floud, the head of the Department, was later appointed my supervisor by Oxford University; Mr. John Lowry supplied useful data on Christopher Dresser and others; and from all the staff I received such kindness and hospitality as made my long visits to London exceptionally agreeable to me. I have also received excellent help from the staffs of the Victoria and Albert Museum Library and the Bodleian Library, Oxford, as well as a number of other persons and institutions.

The printing of the book was made possible through the liberal support of the Norwegian Research Council for Science and the Humanities.

CONTENTS

A FEW
REFLECTIONS

Victorian achievement in the fields of letters and pictorial art has always been generally acknowledged; but since 1900 there have been very few people prepared to praise Victorian furniture, houses and clothes. On the contrary, these products of 19th century civilisation have become almost proverbial for ugliness and lack of taste.

It is perfectly normal that this should be so. In the history of the so-called useful arts, and most clearly maybe in the case of dress, we see again and again how each new generation decries the fashions of yesterday, only to create new ones of its own which in their turn will be obsolete tomorrow, and frequently the objects of ridicule and abuse. The case for rejecting Victorian design, however, has been supported by arguments which refer more particularly to the new industrialism of the age; they may seem to give more weight to the general criticism of what was achieved in the field to be discussed here, and some attention should therefore be paid to them before we enter upon our particular subject.

In the minor arts, Mechanisation became the great watchword as the 19th century advanced, and after, say, 1830 most industries of any importance had been subjected to the machine; workshop production in a craftsmanlike manner was rapidly declining, and with it the artisan's careful personal attention to his particular piece of work. Instead production became systematised on a larger scale than before with insistence on a vast output of impersonal, machine-made series of objects for an anonymous market. At the same time a period of stylistic confusion set in, destined to last the whole century through.

These three principles of *large output of similar pieces*, of *machine-marked goods* and of *stylistic confusion* have been the main arguments for rejecting as works of art the products of Victorian design.

However, on further consideration it will easily be recognised that the conditions prevailing in Victorian times have their roots far back in the 18th century, and that at all events two of the principles just mentioned played a dominant role in fashioning some among the most famous products of the minor arts at that time. Reference may be made for instance to the products of Josiah Wedgwood's potteries in Staffordshire, where in spite of a large output of similar pieces, a high aesthetic standard was secured through the co-operation of renowned artists, who shaped the models from which the important series were made. With regard to another of these principles, an element of stylistic confusion is very markedly present in some of the best of Thomas Chippendale's furniture, to such an extent that Chinese and Gothic elements are frequently seen blended in one and the same piece of an unmistakably rococo character. It seems therefore doubtful whether either of these two factors may in itself be considered degrading.

The stamp of the machine, however, is something genuinely new, the importance of which still remains difficult to judge. One must try, of course, to be impartial in these matters, and it is useful to remember that our present-day feeling for beauty in design is very much influenced by machine-made goods. But it is also true that these to-day are designed on lines which make them eminently fit for machine production, whereas the great mass of Victorian art-manufacture from our present point of view embodied a deceit, in that it simulated the hand-made work of older days. It may be this very incongruity, and what to us seems a lack of honesty and of will to conform to existing facts, which give many among us a feeling of uneasiness when confronted with numerous products of 19th century industrial art; and in that case these feelings *may* be justified. Consideration should also be given to the amount of personal care shown in the detailed execution of design, and here I feel that the difference between the original period piece and its 19th century imitation makes itself most strongly felt. The fact that machines were set to produce forms which were originally designed for execution by hand, did inevitably result in that lack of refinement and of feeling which is so frequently regretted by contemporary observers as well as present-day connoisseurs.

It is difficult to adopt an absolutely objective attitude when judging the art of the Victorian age—or any other age, for that matter; at all times men have been in the habit of favouring some among the older periods in art at the cost of others, and we ourselves are probably bound by the prejudices of our own age as much as any critic of former days. There is one circumstance, however, which may seem to justify a doubt as to the aesthetic value of the greater part of Victorian applied art: this circumstance is to be found in the sociological development of the time.

To turn once more to Josiah Wedgwood, he was born and bred in the order of 18th century England, and he understood the cultural refinement of those people who made up his market at home and abroad; they had a feeling for proportion, for form and finish which he shared, and which was the basis of the critical judgement they jointly brought to bear on the succeeding fashions of the day. It is on this particular point that a change seems to have set in as the 19th century advanced, and "new" people with "new" money came to the front. Their part in creating a new demand for the ostentatious, the vulgarly showy, has been amply stressed by others; but far from sufficient emphasis, I believe, has been laid on the fact that in most cases the manufacturers themselves were also "new" men. They were builders of industry and were highly successful from a commercial point of view, producing as they did for a steadily expanding international market. But they were also men who, unlike Wedgwood, developed their outlook without understanding the

3

predominating spirit among those upper-class people to whom considerations of beauty and style had become part of an attitude to life. And the new leaders of industry could afford to ignore any troublesome ponderings over aesthetics, because to a sufficiently large extent they produced for a public unable thoroughly to understand such matters. Once again, as in the case of Josiah Wedgwood, producer and consumer had found each other—but on what a different basis, and with what different results!

Production, therefore, was carried on as always with an eye to enlarged output and commercial success, *but with small understanding of the problem of taste involved*, and without regard for any sort of moral obligation on the manufacturer's part to produce beautiful wares as well as saleable ones. Together with the stamp of the machine this particular circumstance should be considered the most important reason why Victorian design shows so many unfamiliar traits when compared with that of older times.

I said "the stamp of the machine". Is then the machine product, the typically Victorian piece of design, fundamentally and eternally ugly? That is hard to tell. Taste differs from age to age, but there is at least one consideration which should be borne in mind before pronouncing any final judgement. Strange as it may seem, in spite of our increasing acceptance of machine-made goods even in the minor arts, of which I have spoken already, it is probably true that a great many *critics* until our own day have been in the habit of judging pieces of design according to a pre-industrial standard. True, the predominance of cheap, mass-produced industrial goods has probably robbed the general public of their capacity to judge anything at all; but it is not the general public that writes the books or reviews the exhibits. The people who do that, and the people who at least presume to know, are the art historians, members of museum staffs, or of old or rich families, for whom high quality antiques form part of their daily surroundings. These have influenced their outlook to a very marked extent, and it is a significant fact, to take an example, that until recently only a few museums have shown any interest at all in the typical Victorian *objet d'art*. It is not at all unlikely, therefore, that we have been, and still are, judging Victorian design on the wrong terms, and with a strong bias, if we condemn it. And it may even be that our steadily increasing dependence at present on the machine-made product will gradually change our attitude to the earliest varieties of it in the most fundamental way, or at the very least substantially increase our interest in it as a field of study wherein to achieve a more profound understanding of our own situation in this respect.

The present book deals with an aspect of Victorian applied art which has so far only been skirted by previous writers on the topic. It is a singular fact concerning the design typical of the period that it was disliked not only by the generations following immediately after, but by a great many among the Victorians themselves. It is certainly true that at all times there have been moralists who condemn contemporary ways; but the general opposition shown to the predominant Victorian fashions in design by a fairly large body of artists, craftsmen, and amateurs for three quarters of a century or more is none the less surprising.

However, this dissatisfaction gave rise to a series of reformative movements, which were conducted according to theories more or less elaborately worked out, and more or less firmly expressed. These possess of course great interest in their own right; but when linked up with the entire modern development in the crafts, they acquire an even wider significance: Victorian theories of design point to the conflict which was bound to arise when the established tradition of craftsmanship and workshop manufacture in the crafts was in a comparatively short time broken, and replaced by mechanical mass production on a predominantly commercial basis. The gradual growth of principles to regulate the production of art-manufactures under the new conditions, reflects an increasing concern about the development that was taking place; and the growth of a Victorian theory of design is therefore the story of adjustment to a new and somewhat perplexing state of affairs.

In the following pages I have tried to give an account of the main tendencies in theoretical development from the early years of the Queen's reign until almost the last years of the century. The pieces actually produced during this period have only interested me in so far as they conform to expressed ideas; it must be quite clear, therefore, that what I have written will give an extremely one-sided picture of the development of design itself; this partly because the most outstanding propagator of ideas is not always the best artist, but also because the larger part of Victorian design was probably executed without any reference whatever to the more advanced ideas of the time. I feel justified, however, in treating ideas largely in independence of the artistic forms which once embodied them, because of that independent life which ideas always tend to lead. In this particular case they have achieved a widespread influence in more recent times, acting as a leaven in the Continental movement of *Art Nouveau* and contributing to the *Bauhaus* movement in Germany before Hitler's accession to power.

Some apology should perhaps be made for what may seem an excessive use of quotations in the text. I have, however, wanted not only to give a full documentation of my own statements, but also to bring to light as fully as possible material not easily accessible outside the most central libraries in Britain.

I offer my little book to the public in the hope that they may share some of the pleasure I have myself felt in writing it.

THE BACKGROUND

*Early Victorian Commercial Design
in the Great Exhibition of 1851*

So far Victorian art-manufacture has been spoken of without reference to a single example. Before embarking upon the study of theories put forth to improve it, I therefore believe it helpful to assert by way of example some of its most striking characteristics. In doing this, I shall not bring forward anything essentially new, and the following survey largely follows the paths trodden by others.[1] It is, however, indispensable as a background for our particular study, and with a few reservations some objects chosen from among the exhibits of the Great Exhibition of 1851 will have to serve the purpose.

The reservations are these: we have every reason to believe that industrial design in 1851 did not in its general characteristics differ essentially from what existed let us say ten years before, by which date the new tendencies must have firmly asserted themselves. Even so, it is hardly safe to take the exhibits of '51 as an altogether undisputed guide to early Victorian taste, because it is evident that they were to a large extent show-pieces, many of them far removed from the more even tenor of everyday requirements, even of the wealthier part of the upper classes. Many were curiosities, certainly understood and estimated as such even by the Victorians themselves, and finally the taste shown at the Exhibition was severely criticised

7

from various quarters at the time. It seems therefore on the whole more fair to suggest that the Exhibition provides illustrations of what happened when certain predominant tendencies were given free rein so that industry might create without even the smallest consideration of cost and utility.

However, when all allowances have been made, exhibits at the Great Exhibition may still be considered as illustrating the tendencies against which reform was directed; and so a closer study of them remains indispensable to anyone who wants to reach a just estimation of the various efforts made to turn the tide of public taste and improve the standard of design. The *Great Exhibition Official Catalogue*, the *Art Journal Exhibition Volume*, and the *Illustrated London News* are well-known sources which will give the best understanding of 1851, its tendencies and characteristics.

When turning these pages, it becomes immediately obvious that the battle of the styles—or maybe rather a happy fraternisation between them—is one of the predominant features of 1851. Most wares with the smallest claim to artistic appearance are seen adorned with the ornamental garb of one or more of the stylistic "periods", and we find a profusion of objects of the most varied functions decorated in the greatest variety of style; by way of example may be cited a very complicated clock in something which may best be described as Elizabethan, adorned with allegoric figures, and with some sort of Gothic structure inside it *(Fig. 1)*. There are also some electric telegraphs with Gothic finials and ogee arches, or shaped like a classical temple front *(Fig. 2)*, and various pieces of furniture, like "Erard's Elizabethan New Patent Grand Oblique Piano-forte" *(Fig. 3)*, or "Carved and gilt Console Table and Frame, with Pier Glass", in the "Louis XIV style" *(Fig. 4)*. Other examples are only too numerous, and one is almost led to believe that only in objects with no claim to artistic beauty, was a shape sometimes adopted with the sole end in view of making that object serve its purpose. This is the case with most machinery in the Exhibition, and with prosaic objects like invalid chairs and kitchen stoves. Here many examples may be found of straightforward functional design *(Fig. 5)*.

The period styles were also made to adapt themselves to new materials and to objects of new invention; in furniture and the like, wood was frequently replaced by iron, cast or wrought into rococo shapes; and even the functional line of an engine might occasionally be scorned in preference for a Gothic mould. Judged according to pre-industrial conventions, such devices must seem entirely out of place, as they tend to result in unhappy relations between form and function on the one hand, and material, weight, and methods of production on the other. However, such considerations do not seem to have troubled the Victorians themselves at that stage.

We have also ample reason to believe that their actual knowledge of styles and stylistic development was, at least as compared with present standards, very far from first class.[2]

A somewhat indiscriminate adaptation of period styles to modern materials and objects of modern use is then our first characteristic of Victorian design. The second consists in the *mixing* of styles— not only from one room to another, but within the same room, and even within one and the same object, as has already been seen in *Fig. 1*, with the Gothic belfry placed inside an Elizabethan clock.

Besides this tendency to stylistic imitation, Nikolaus Pevsner has pointed to a certain bulginess which he considers among the chief characteristics of the time: "all curves are eminently generous, all outlines broken or blurred." "A universal replacement of the straight line by the curve is one of the chief characteristics of mid-Victorian design ... generous, full or ... bulgy."[3] These characteristics, found in several of the objects illustrated here, are taken by Pevsner to express the self-satisfaction and the comfortable plenitude of mid-Victorian bourgeois life.

Among other strongly marked characteristics is a *horror vacui* which tends to cover empty spaces with ornaments of all kinds (see *Figs. 1, 3*, and *4);* these would as a rule be borrowed from the style of one or more periods, and show an eminent lack of power or will

9

to discriminate between the various ornamental elements within one style. Frequently they are all employed simultaneously, crammed together in one and the same object. In *Fig. 4*, for instance, the mirror according to the catalogue is Louis XIV, while to us it seems to be built up of elements taken from a fully developed rococo style. If it were to be rococo, however, the strict symmetry of the candlesticks and of the ornaments on both sides of the glass would seem to be inappropriate, and so would the arrangement of rocailles, for instance, between the legs and the top of the console table. Another typical Victorian feature is the title given to this piece of furniture; it was called "The Genius of Commerce", and at the top we see this genius in the form of a naked putto with pawing winged horses on both sides. Of this preference for narrative elements and symbols, more will be said presently.

This profusion of ornament may more often than not be executed with a certain coarseness which becomes apparent on a closer examination of the objects; this was probably the result of impersonal mass production and factory labour, and, as it seems, gave no reason for offence to the general public. This tendency is of course not universally noticeable, but may be easily demonstrated for instance in ornamental cast-iron work: here the feeling for *finesse* and delicacy barely asserts itself; the outlines are blurred, and the forms doughy.

The interest in the narrative element of art pointed out in connection with the console mirror frame, may be easily recognized in contemporary sculpture and painting as well as in articles in everyday use. At the Great Exhibition, Arthur J. Jones, Dublin, exhibited "Series of Irish bog-yew decorative furniture, designed to illustrate the history, antiquities, animal and vegetable productions, etc., of Ireland"—in 18 pieces. Among a profusion of symbolic and allegoric figures and scenes on the legs of tables and the backs of chairs, or in similar appropriate places, may be mentioned by way of example "a group representing the destruction of the wolf by the Irish wolf-dog", "a figure of Commerce .... surrounded by the

exports of Ireland", a "wine-table, supported by the harp of Brian
Boru and Bacchanalian standards", and finally a chair with a sleeping
and a watching dog for armrests, and the mottoes "Gentle when
stroked" and "Fierce when provoked" on their respective collars.[4]
Other examples might be quoted by the hundred—a "gladiator
table, the pillar represents a fighting gladiator carved in solid Irish
oak", or a "sideboard supported on two cornucopias and dolphins'
heads, which are carved with fruit, flowers, and figures representing Youth and Old Age", and a Bacchus, with palms, vine, hop, and
oak, and with the hounds and the wild boar on each side.[5] A final
example, from the *Illustrated London News*,[6] shows this tendency
to the full: it consists of a

> ... magnificent centre ornament and *plateau*, by Messrs. Hunt and Roskell, ...
> It is adapted as a stand for flowers by day, and as a candelabrum by night; and
> with these objects the various groups are selected to agree in subject. On each
> quarter of the *plateau* are groups representing the seasons: Flora, attended by
> her nymphs, playing with flowers, and a lamb, personifying Spring, Zephyrs,
> bearing on their shoulders a female figure, crowned with wheat, and carrying
> the sickle, representing Summer. Autumn is typified by the figures of Silenus,
> Bacchus, and Pomona. Winter by aged Saturnus, who, seated on a leafless tree,
> spreads his mantle over shivering nature. On his left is a figure representing
> storm and tempest, accompanied by wolves. Beneath the groups are the signs of
> the Zodiac. On the foot of the centre ornament are figures representing the
> quarters of the world, each being accompanied by appropriate animals. The
> alto-relievo around the column represents Day and Night, attended by the
> Hours; and around the stem which supports the vase are four figures, represent-
> ing the elements. The whole is richly decorated with ornament of the *Cinque
> Cento* period.

In their love for allegory and story-telling the Victorians do not
of course stand alone; the element of narration has been strongly
stressed in the art of all times and of all peoples, with very few
exceptions—one of which I hold to be certain aspects of 20th century
European art. Already in the latter half of the 19th century, however,
James McNeil Whistler ridiculed the typical English painter because
he paid more attention to his *subject* than to his display of artistic
genius in rendering it; at the period when Sir J. E. Millais painted

the *North West Passage* and *Bubbles Bursting*, Whistler produced his series of *Harmonies* and *Nocturnes*, adapting abstract terms of music to the aesthetics of canvas, brush, and paint. To-day, of course, painters have completely removed the narrative element from their pictures, while the functionalists have stripped architecture of statues and reliefs moulded in plaster or cut in stone on facades of houses; in so doing they have waged war on old-time putti, amorini, flowers, birds, and beasts with which the interiors, the dress, the furniture, the cups and vases of our grandparents were so profusely adorned. The early Victorian love of narrative ornament, therefore, assumes its high interest first and foremost in relation to what occurred half a century later, when tendencies which had their birth in the latter half of the 19th century sprang fully into view. We shall see later how as a matter of fact full-fledged functionalism in design developed already in Victorian times.

However, in 1851 the allegoric element held the field, and was even considered by the jurors to be a point of special importance. Speaking of Sculpture, Models, and objects of the Plastic Arts, it is stated that "the reward will have reference ... in the case of models to the interest attached to the subject they represent".[7]

No less striking than the tendency towards stylistic imitation and the interest in *Subject* was a keen delight in minute imitation of nature; hence a series of cups, vases, dessert stands, etc., ornamented or built up like flowers or knots of leaves and stalks with minute naturalistic imitations of men and animals. *(Figs. 6, 7)*. This was indeed a very prominent feature in mid-Victorian design, and not restricted to design only. In his defence of the Pre-Raphaelites John Ruskin praised them for accurate imitation of flowers,[8] and some years later he encouraged the workmen at the Oxford Museum to carve leaves and grass from nature on their sandstone capitals in the interior of the building.[9] Numerous passages from contemporary writers in the *Art Journal*, for instance, stress the same point, and vegetable design copied in close imitation of nature had come to be used increasingly in textiles and in other flat designs such as wallpapers; these show flowers, leaves, grass, and sometimes whole landscapes in perspective and with shaded colours, to such an extent as to achieve an altogether illusionistic effect.

Again, this is not a feature which is likely to surprise anyone who possesses some knowledge of the history of design. Close study of the details of organic life, even to the point of copying many of them for ornamental purposes by means of casts, is a well-known practice in Western art: the famous Palissy-ware with its strikingly naturalistic insects and reptiles, is a case in point. The naturalism of early Victorian times forms in many ways a continuation of strongly asserted 18th century tendencies, when representations of eatables would very appropriately be moulded on pieces of table silver, alternating with illustrations of classical myths in relief, incised, or in the round. Even the sober products of neo-classicism are by no means free from this.

All the same, Victorian naturalism seems to me to possess special characteristics of its own. First, it is much more widely applied, frequently even in places where it must seriously detract from the usefulness of an object adorned in this way. Next, because a strong note of sentimentality so frequently seems to prevail, as for instance in a table centre of silver gilt made in 1842 by *Robert Garrard* for the Queen, after a design by Prince Albert: here

Models of four favourite dogs of Queen Victoria are placed on a circular plateau, namely a greyhound Eos, a Skye terrier Cairnach, a rough-haired terrier Islay, and a dachshund Waldmann. The dogs' names are inscribed on a square pedestal . . .

and evidently without the least sense of incongruity, these pets have been honoured with the presence of the engraved royal arms and ciphers of Queen Victoria and the Prince Consort.[10] Lastly, Victorian naturalism in design seems frequently to be the outcome of a strong scientific interest in natural phenomena; this, we must remember, was the age of the lady mineral-collector, and of the serious adolescent student of botany and zoology. The Prince Consort himself is a good case in point, and in the field of art criticism John Ruskin tried to establish a canon of judgement based on a kind of divinely inspired study of forms in nature. In his dissertations on art he frequently mixes scientific observation of this kind with sentiment in the most extraordinary fashion.

In yet another respect the Great Exhibition of 1851 carries on and expands a practice already firmly established in 18th century English design. Most connoisseurs will regard with admiration and delight the ingenious devices by which furniture of that age has been made to serve several different ends—how small mahogany commodes may expand into elaborate combinations of writing-table and toilet-table, how card-tables and dinner-tables fold up until they take up next to no room, and so on. Similarly, the technical outlook of the Victorian age was manifest not only in the vast exhibits of machinery and objects of practical use, but also in a certain pleasure in intricate technical niceties such as in the follow-ing example chosen among furniture and upholstery: "Table, con-vertible into a bedstead"; "Patent Ottoman, convertible into a chair"; "A patent circular dining-table, made on a simple principle, to expand from a small to a large size, without the aid of spring or fastening, in mahogany"; "Patented suspensory chair, forming a couch or camp bed. Adapting itself to every movement of the body"; "Portable expanding chair, of cane and English ash. By moving the thumb-screw in the seat, it is raised to any suitable height; by moving the other screw, it is made to fold up altogether"; "Circular revolving dining-table, of walnut, with portable sweet-flaps; the centre part revolves, while the outside portion, or flaps, remain stationary".[11] In other classes, more easily given over to the genius of the inventor, the tendency was still more developed. But even in furniture and objects designed for interior decoration and furnishing these and similar devices are so numerous that it seems justifiable to consider *inventiveness* to be an important characteristic in Victorian design. This is shown even in the falsification of material: several of the exhibiting firms show "specimens of painting, in imitation of various marbles .... Intended as a substitute for marble in the construction of chimney-pieces, inlaying of tables, etc. Painting, in imitation of oak"; "Panel in imitation of inlaid wood, for doors of drawing-rooms and decorated apartments"; "Specimens on slate, in imitation of China"; "Imitation of various woods, in painting"; "Imitation of inlaid marbles, in wood decorations and table tops"; we also find *papier maché* disguised as lacquer work with inlaid mother-of-pearl, bronzed cast iron, etc., etc.[12] The significant point in this connection, however, is that this kind of imitation was not at all considered a thing to be ashamed of or to be concealed: it was on the contrary thought highly clever, if not even desirable—as when, in the *Illustrated London News*, we find an illustration of a "wall decoration", the "end of a drawingroom in the Elizabethan style. The fittings, glass frame, and exquisite chimney-piece containing a medallion of Chaucer, and groups from his most celebrated poems, are by Mr. Thomas, whose fertile genius has so much enriched the New Palace at Westminster". Then follows an elaborate description of the effect of the various materials used, which are, among others, white marble, giallo antico, and "sparkling gems of lapis lazuli, malachite, and rubies, and inlaid gold". Further, we find jasper, gritto, and various coloured grounds, seemingly rich enough to rival any palace from the Arabian Nights. Then, at the end, we are told that

It is impossible by engravings to represent the beautiful colours, the richness and marvellous transparency of these imitations of marbles, in which Mr. Moxon has rivalled the varied tints of nature with great fidelity, and this novel application of painted mosaic for decorative purposes may be considered perfectly successful.[13]

Here can be traced no feeling of deceit or cheating, only pride in the advance of scientific knowledge and technical skill.

By way of general observation it should finally be noted that the tendency to decorate more often than not is stronger than the will to create objects of a merely constructive and practical form. *Ornamental* was the catchword in this respect, and commentators in the *Art Journal* and elsewhere write of ornamental inkstands and ornamental coal-scuttles and ornamental this and that, and frequently illustrate with examples that seem quite impossible from a practical point of view. In the eye of a modern functionalist, those objects therefore seem most attractive that have been built first and foremost to be used, without consideration of a representative appearance. In them practical considerations have sometimes imposed a check alike on decoration and on falsification of material. Machinery and kitchen stoves have been mentioned before in this connection, and other examples may be furnished by horse-carriages, weapons, and the like.

If some general conclusions may be drawn from cursory observations like those above, it seems that the most outstanding characteristics of Victorian design as shown in the Great Exhibition of 1851 were as follows:

1. Tendency to imitate or to be inspired by older styles.
2. Tendency to free, undiscriminating application of period styles, for instance so as to mix elements from several styles in one and the same place, or overcrowd with ornament, or apply the wrong ornament in the wrong place.
3. Coarseness and lack of formal refinement, involving what may seem too profuse a use of ornament. Partiality to bulgy, curved forms.
4. Overpowering interest in a narrative and allegoric form of decoration, frequently manifesting itself in the adoption of classical myth. There is a strong tendency to sentimentality.
5. Ornament is designed in close imitation of natural form, frequently in a scientific spirit. Artificial imitation of genuine materials universally adopted.
6. There is a strong pride in inventive, technical skill such as various practical devices in the design of furniture. In spite of this, the next point is none the less true, that
7. The interest in functional and structural form is less marked than the tendency to decorate.

In short, this was an art of design which for its effects relied mainly on imitation and on narrative, associative elements. Novelty and enterprise were shown in technical, not in artistic matters; execution, even when technically perfect, more often than not lacked formal refinement and careful attention to detail.

Such then were the characteristics against which the criticism of the time itself was directed; and we shall now pass on to the men who most strongly felt the need for improvement, and to the theories which they advanced with that end in view.

II

GOTHIC REFORM

August Northmore Welby Pugin

England was probably the first country in Europe to be concerned about the conditions of her arts and crafts as related to the influences now brought to bear on them—as was natural enough, since in Britain those industries reached a high degree of importance at an early date. If— for thoroughness' sake—we go to the root of things, we find a "Royal Society of Arts" founded in 1754, "for the Encouragement of Arts, Manufacture, and Commerce",[1] and at Edinburgh, in 1760, the Board of Manufacturers started a school "to promote the art of drawing for the use of manufactures (linen and wool mainly)".[2] But these must have been little more than voices in the wilderness, with no noticeable importance and effect; and another 75 years elapsed, in the course of which the manufacturing of British ceramics, among other things, reached its last high peak of excellence before the Victorian era, while the Gothic Revival developed from the whimsical fancy of amateurs at Strawberry Hill and Fonthill Abbey to be a style employed in all seriousness by architects who studied it with much care in every detail. Books with plans and ornamental details appeared in increasing numbers to promote its correct application, among them Augustus Pugin's *Specimens of Gothic Architecture*, which was published in two volumes in 1820 and 1827. In 1831 he brought out his *Examples of Gothic Architecture*, the second volume of which appeared five years later.

The first noticeable efforts towards a consistent theory of formal art-values in their relation to art-manufacture, appeared in this very connection. In the introduction to the 1836 volume of Pugin's *Examples* one reads the statement that

a servile adhesion to ancient models, exclusive of all invention, cannot reasonably be required. Modern edifices must be adapted to modern habits of life, and the wants and wishes of the present generation.

Needless to say, the adaptation here spoken of was an adaptation of *Gothic* architecture, and we must not therefore allow ourselves to believe that with this very modern-sounding piece of advice we stand at the fountain-head of 20th century functionalism: the quotation may not safely be taken to indicate anything more than that its author was aware of certain material differences between the 13th and the 19th centuries. However, when all has been said, this pronouncement marks at least a noteworthy development in the history of the Gothic Revival itself, where from now on a retrospective interest in its archaeological and romantic aspects gave room beside it for practical considerations concerning the material needs of the 19th century.

The significant lines—since, after all, significant they were—were written by Pugin's friend and collaborator Edward James Willson; they heralded a new phase in architectural criticism, in which the most prominent figure was to be Pugin's very remarkable son, the Catholic and Gothic architect August Northmore Welby Pugin, who edited the work for publication after his father's death in 1832. This younger Pugin's fame was great and widespread in his own day, but was for a long time dimmed by the overshadowing position of John Ruskin from the 'fifties onwards—and most likely by Protestant prejudices on the part of the public as well. It has been left to the present generation of critics to place him in the undisputed position of a forerunner of modern ideas, and an innovator of architectural principles of the very first order.[3]

It sounds too much like a cliché, but it is none the less true that there was something Byronic in Pugin's character. Precocious,

19

vehement, pushing on with tremendous energy, unorthodox in habits, speech, and manners, he was essentially a Romantic of the more fullblooded type in his tastes and prejudices, as well as in the visible and outward characteristics of his career. Born in 1812, he was employed as a designer at the age of fifteen, drawing furniture and interior fittings for Windsor Castle. For two years he worked as a stage designer at Covent Garden, and by 1832 he had failed at running a workshop for the production of Gothic ornament, and became a bankrupt—all at the age of twenty.

Into the short span of forty years—he died in 1852—he crammed three marriages with eight children, and, besides, two unsuccessful courtships; he wrote a number of books that were to influence his contemporaries in the most profound manner and carry architectural criticism to the threshold of our own era; he travelled widely on the Continent, read extensively, and carried on a large practice as an architect—building churches and castles all over the country as well as two houses for himself. One of his most conspicuous and best known works is the decorative detail, at least, of Barry's Houses of Parliament.[4]

According to his earliest biographer,[5] Pugin's early literary interests embraced a mediaeval taste for romances and tales of mystery, coupled with an overpowering interest in Gothic architecture; this he fed through literary studies and youthful excavations of the foundations of Rochester Castle, and carried with him to the theatrical world of Covent Garden, where he designed stage-settings "in the mediaeval style", and achieved "great success" in correcting "errors in judgement" on the part of contemporary stage designers. His passion for the theatre at this time also made him convert the attic of his father's house into a model stage of his own, equipped with complete and highly complicated stage machinery.

Most probably, this all-absorbing interest in mediaevalism and in theatrical picturesqueness was instrumental in bringing Pugin over to the Catholic Church, where he soon became prominent among the *avant-gardistes* of its revival. Pugin held that Gothic architecture and art had been developed to answer the need of a Catholic world, and simple logic told him that the one could not go on living without the other. In this sociological approach to art, it is easily seen how he antedates Ruskin by roughly fifteen years.

His formal conversion took place in 1835,[6] and in the next year he published the work which was to bring him into the public eye as a champion of a Catholic Gothic Revival, and which also marks an epoch in the history of art criticism; this work was the much celebrated *Contrasts*.[7] This slim volume of 58 pages with another 46 pages of appendices contains 19 engraved plates of illustration, which—with somewhat exaggerated unfairness—compare corresponding specimens of mediaeval and contemporary architecture, to the carefully planned disadvantage of the latter. The long appendices contain quotations of sources and incidents to demonstrate the utter viciousness and criminality of the Reformers in England and, altogether, the book forms a surprising piece of Catholic propaganda.

"On comparing the Architectural Works of the last three Centuries with those of the Middle Ages, the wonderful superiority of the latter must strike every attentive observer". These are the opening words of Pugin's *Contrasts*. In the reasons he gave for this preference, no mention is at this stage made of structural advantages to be found in the Gothic style; the entire argument is in favour of it because "Pointed or Christian Architecture has far higher claims on our admiration than mere beauty or antiquity; .... in it alone we find *the faith of Christianity embodied, and its practices illustrated.*" To follow Pugin in more detail:

The three great doctrines, of the redemption of man by the sacrifice of our Lord on the cross; the three equal persons united in one Godhead; and the resurrection of the dead,—are the foundation of Christian Architecture.

The first—the cross—is not only the very plan and form of a Catholic church, but it terminates each spire and gable, and is imprinted as a seal of faith on the very furniture of the altar.

The second is fully developed in the triangular form and arrangement of arches, tracery, and even subdivisions of the buildings themselves.

The third is beautifully exemplified by great height and vertical lines, which have been considered by the Christians, from the earliest period, as the emblem of the resurrection.

On this last account he also reasons that one may consider

the introduction of the depressed or four-centred arch as the first symptom of the decline of Christian Architecture, the leading character of which was the vertical or pointed principle.[8]

I can see no objection to concluding from this that Pugin's preference for Gothic was directed, in its early stages, by an interest in its symbolic or narrative interests closely akin to what we found typical of the mid-Victorian approach as illustrated in the Great Exhibition. Also, the dignity of religious life which it represented appealed strongly to the Catholic convert, as, for instance, when he contrasted a mediaeval and a contemporary episcopal residence *(Fig. 8):* the one speaking of a life of devotion and pious study, meditation, and hospitable charity, with a communal life symbolised by the great Hall; the other, one among a row of similarly shaped bourgeois houses, like them fitted out exclusively for the private comfort of its owner, and in an architectural style which to Pugin symbolised a return to the worldliness of heathen times.

His love for Gothic was also increased through the sentimental human qualities he found embedded in it, as when he ascribes its excellence to the spiritual attitude of those who built in the Middle Ages. Describing in vivid terms the beauties of a Catholic Gothic cathedral—the description sounds almost like a stage-set for a theatrical play— he states that

Such effects as these can only be produced on the mind by buildings, the composition of which has emanated from men who were thoroughly embued with devotion for, and faith in, the religion for whose worship they were erected . . . . They felt they were engaged in one of the most glorious occupations that can fall to the lot of man—that of raising a temple to the worship of the true and living God.

It was this feeling that operated alike on the master-mind that planned the edifice, and on the patient sculptor whose chisel wrought each varied and beautiful detail... and it is a feeling that may be traced throughout the

22

whole of the numerous edifices of the middle ages, and which, amidst the great variety of genius which their varied decorations display, still bespeaks the unity of purpose which influenced their builders and artists.[9]

Much of this seems familiar—but from a later, not an earlier source. Pugin anticipated Ruskin in his remarks on the depressed arch, which initiated a valuation of various Gothic periods according to certain moral considerations. Likewise, when he praised Gothic building on account of the feeling of the workmen which he found it expressed, he more than suggested a line of thought which Ruskin was to develop in *Stones of Venice*.

Finally, Ruskin's interpretation of the transition from Gothic to Renaissance, involving a parallel between artistic decline in architecture, and moral corruption in society, was grasped one and a half decades earlier by Pugin, who wrote that

Christian art was the natural result of the progress of Catholic feeling and devotion; and its decay was consequent on that of the faith itself; and all revived classic buildings, whether erected in Catholic or Protestant countries, are evidences of a lamentable departure from true Catholic principles and feelings.

Classical art and Paganism were synonyms to Pugin, both objectionable on moral grounds. Contrary to Gothic, which arose in a spirit of sacrifice and devotion, classic art was sought by "almost all the celebrated artists of the last three centuries .... for a display of their art and the increase of fame."

Again like Ruskin, Pugin was no advocate of "Art for Art's sake". Art and religion should speak with one voice:

What madness, then, while neglecting our own religious and national types of architecture and art, to worship at the revived shrines of ancient corruption, and profane the temple of a crucified Redeemer by the architecture and emblems of heathen gods.[10]

The point was taken up again in his next book, *The True Principles of Pointed or Christian Architecture* (1841):

It is .... essential to ecclesiastical propriety that the ornaments introduced about churches should be appropriate and significant .... Is our wisdom set

3   23

forth by the owl of Minerva, or our strength by the club of Hercules? ....
Let us away with such gross inconsistencies, and restore the Christian ideas of
our Catholic ancestors, for they alone are proper for our imitation.[11]

The religious side to Pugin's line of argument goes to prove how
many elements other than purely practical and aesthetic ones were
brought to bear on a consideration of the arts by the Victorian mind.
Not that Pugin lacked a truly professional eye for architecture and
its structural principles: his importance as a theoretician rests
primarily on his consideration of this side of the question.

It can by now hardly seem surprising that this aspect of his
criticism also developed along Gothic lines; it is most likely that
his early sympathy for Gothic preceded any theoretical valuation of
its practical qualities, and that Pugin's theoretical speculation as to
structural fitness, for instance, was in some measure a late attempt
firmly to justify his youthful love—at the same time, of course,
finding room for his prejudice against classical architecture. The
latter he found technically deceitful and structurally unsound,
as in the Greek temple, which, originally a wooden structure, was
transformed into stone without "the *properties of this material*"
suggesting to the builders "*some different and improved mode of
construction*", so that, in fact, "the finest temple of the Greeks is
constructed on the *same principle* as a large wooden cabin." Christian architects, on the contrary, took full account of the possibilities
of the material they used, and

during the *dark ages,* with stone scarcely larger than ordinary bricks, threw
their lofty vaults from slender pillars across a vast intermediate space, and that
at an amazing height, where they had every difficulty of lateral pressure to
contend with.

And so, on point after point, Pugin goes on, all through the first
part of his *Principles,* to demonstrate the practical and structural
soundness, and consequent superiority, of Gothic building: for
instance, the buttresses, in Gothic architecture frankly exhibited
and beautified constructive members, are in the classical St. Paul's
deceitfully "*concealed by an enormous screen .... so that in*

fact one half of the edifice is built to conceal the other[12] — a sin against the principle that "architectural skill consists in embodying and expressing the structure required, and not in disguising it by borrowed features."[13]Similar comparisons are made for other architectural members—flying buttresses, pinnacles and spiral terminations, high-pitched roofs which are made "sufficiently steep to throw off snow without giving the slate or lead covering *too perpendicular a strain"*, and so on. And scattered throughout the book are a number of broad abstract principles with a surprisingly modern ring, such as,

The two great rules for design are these: *1st, that there should be no features about a building which are not necessary for convenience, construction, or propriety; 2nd, that all ornament should consist of enrichment of the essential construction of the building.*

.... the smallest detail should *have a meaning or serve a purpose;* and even the construction itself *should vary with the material employed,* and the designs should be adapted to the material in which they are executed.

As to

decoration with reference to propriety ... *the external and internal appearance of an edifice should be illustrative of, and in accordance with, the purpose for which it is destined.* There is a vast difference between a building raised to God and one for temporal purposes.

It is, of course, "strange as it may appear at first sight ... in *pointed architecture alone that these great principles have been carried out."*

Among the many pitfalls which threatened the modern architect was the temptation to replace some strong and durable material by a cheaper substitute; for this practice Pugin had nothing but contempt: "as for plaster, when used for any other purpose than coating walls, it is a mere modern deception, and the trade is not worthy of a distinction."[14] "Cast-iron is a deception; it is seldom or never left as iron. It is disguised by paint, either as stone, wood, or marble."—"*Wooden groining* is decidedly bad, because it is employing a material *in the place and after the manner of stone, which requires an entirely different mode of construction."* Altogether, the severity of Christian or Pointed Architecture is utterly opposed to all deception: better is it to do a little substantially and consistently with truth than to produce a great but false show. Cheap deceptions of magnificence encourage persons to assume a semblance of decoration far beyond either their means or their station . . . . Glaring, showy, and meretricious ornament was never so much in vogue as at present; it disgraces every branch of our art and manufactures, and the correction of it should be an earnest consideration with every person who desires to see the real principles of art restored.

It is consequently not to be expected that Pugin should be an enthusiastic champion of even Gothic architecture in his time—and indeed he was not. Imitation of foreign styles he cared for little enough—"we are not Italians..."—and if for no other reason, Italian architecture is made for another climate, which "we cannot fortunately import... with its architecture". However,

those who profess to admire pointed architecture, and who strive to imitate it, produce more ridiculous results than those who fly to foreign aid. What can be more absurd than houses built in what is termed the castellated style? .... [this] originated in the wants consequent on a certain state of society .... as models for our imitation they are worse than useless. What absurdities, what anomalies, what utter contradictions do not the builders of modern castles perpetrate! How many portcullises which will not lower down, and drawbridges which will not draw up.... watch-towers, where the housemaids sleep, and a bastion in which the butler cleans his plate: all is a mere mask, and the whole building an ill-conceived lie.

He thought no better of the so-called Abbey-style, and quoted Fonthill as a bad example. He held it a general error with Gothic builders that their houses were *"designed to be picturesque"*, whereas *"The picturesque effect of the ancient buildings results from the ingenious methods by which the old builders overcame local and constructive difficulties"*. Consequently,

An architect should exhibit his skill by turning the difficulties which occur in raising an elevation from *a convenient plan* into so many *picturesque beauties;* and this constitutes the great difference between the principles of classic and pointed domestic architecture. In the former *he would be compelled to devise expedients to conceal these irregularities;* in the latter *he has only to beautify them.*

26

And all inconsistencies in this respect "have arisen from this great error,—*the plans of buildings are designed to suit the elevation, instead of the elevation being made subservient to the plan.*"[15]

Apparently sound rules, not always followed by Pugin in his own practice, it is true, but important none the less. They indicate a thorough understanding of the more prosaic elements of building, based on the demand for convenience and practical utility; preferring to a formal and representative exterior design the more wayward pleasure of the picturesque, reading in its walls the history of an edifice, with the architect's struggles, his victories and defeats. Unhampered individuality and opposition to formal rules were architectural principles which well suited the unconventional attitude of a man who more than a century ago travelled about the country on commissions dressed like a sailor, who despised the monotony of formal dress, and received honoured guests at his door clad in breeches, silk stockings, and a velvet cloak, holding a silver candlestick in his hand, with servants in attendance behind. He must have possessed, on the whole, an extraordinary feeling for quality and beauty in objects and life generally, never in personal habits and appearance giving way to conventional inconveniences which thwarted it. In this as in many other respects there are striking parallels between Pugin and the later William Morris—both extremely emphatic natures, artistic, unconventional, but warm-hearted, with strong social instincts. They possessed a common background in the Gothic Revival, and both eventually carried on a large business as designers and producers of furniture and articles for interior decoration. It is regrettable that little is known which makes it possible to link up with each other these two most gifted among the decorative artists of the Victorian Age.

Pugin was no less outstanding as a designer in the ordinary sense of the word than as an architect, and his theories embrace both fields: his architectural principles are relevant, as far as they may be applied, to design and art-manufactures also. His remarks concerning the lesser arts are without exception in keeping with his views as an architect, and equally significant. Again he is the champion of a reasoned and functional mediaeval style. The illustration given in *Fig. 9* "of the extravagant style of Modern Gothic Furniture and Decoration" is taken from his own *True Principles of Pointed or Christian Architecture*, where his scornful comment runs as follows:

Were the real principles of Gothic architecture restored, the present objection of its extreme costliness would cease to exist. In pointed decoration *too much* is generally attempted.

Interiors .... are one mass of elaborate work; there is no repose, no solidity, no space left for hangings or simple panels: the whole is covered with trifling details, enormously expensive, and at the same time subversive of good effect. These observations apply equally to furniture;—upholsterers seem to think that nothing can be Gothic unless it is found in some church .... We find diminutive flying buttresses about an arm-chair; every thing is crocketed with angular projections, innumerable mitres, sharp ornaments, and turreted extremities. A man who remains any length of time in a modern Gothic room, and escapes without being wounded by some of its minutiae, may consider himself extremely fortunate.

He laments

the inconsistencies of modern grates, which are not unfrequently made to represent diminutive fronts of castellated or ecclesiastical buildings with turrets, loopholes, windows, and doorways, all in a space of forty inches.

In short,

It is impossible to enumerate half the absurdities of modern metal-workers; but all these proceed from the false notion of *disguising* instead of *beautifying* articles of utility. How many objects of ordinary use are rendered monstrous and ridiculous because the artist, instead of seeking the *most convenient form*, and *then decorating it,* has embodied some extravagance *to conceal the real purpose for which the article has been made!*

Worst of all are

those inexhaustible mines of bad taste, Birmingham and Sheffield: staircase turrets for inkstands, monumental crosses for light-shades, gable ends hung on handles for door-porters, and four doorways and a cluster of pillars to support a French lamp .... Neither relative scale, form, purpose, nor unity of style, is ever considered by those who design these abominations.[16]

I have quoted Pugin thus fully on this point because of the particular interest we may well assign to his comments on a style of which nowadays very little is known outside ecclesiastical buildings.

His own broad principles concerning decorative detail were formulated in the introduction to his *Glossary of Ecclesiastical Ornament* (1844), where in the preface he defines "Ornament, in the true
and proper meaning of the word" as "the embellishment of that
which is in itself useful, in an appropriate manner". From this
"appropriate" he excludes "mere enrichment", "unmeaning detail",
because

Every ornament, to deserve the name, must *possess an appropriate meaning,*
and be *introduced with an intelligent purpose,* and on *reasonable grounds.*
The symbolical associations of each ornament must be understood and considered: otherwise things beautiful in themselves will be rendered absurd by
their application .... it is not possible for any forms or enrichments to be
ornamental that are not *appropriate* and *significant,* if their utility extends
no farther.

The stress on symbolic appropriateness is by now familiar to us, and
should be given due notice; although in view of Pugin's well-known
artistic gifts it is absurd to conclude that he did not also possess an
eye for pure abstract values of colour and form, it is well to be aware
that many of his statements which seemingly relate to these values
in reality have what I am—by now—tempted to call a typical Victorian reading. Thus, when Pugin in the same place writes that "it has
been said poetically, that 'Where use is exiled, beauty scorns to dwell:'
and the sentiment is formed in truth and reason", then the modern
reader says to himself, "Ah, Pugin—the advocate of a functionalistic
theory of beauty: the Victorian Corbusier!"—whereas it is perfectly
clear from the context that "use" refers to the correct, appropriate
use of ornament, so that its meaning shall conform to the use or
character of the object for which it is made. Nor should a modern
enthusiast overlook the manner in which his hero constantly refers
to ornament and decoration as something added to, and stuck on,
the finished object. Certainly, Pugin's practice gives ample proof
that he had a well-developed sense for unity of effect, and knew
how to compose and distribute ornamental form to make up a decorative unity with the object he set out to adorn; but from his writings
as well as from his works, it seems evident that his (again Victorian?)

love for ornament for its own sake would leave him a stranger to our modern conception of a supreme beauty dependent on pure functional form.

Pugin seems to be the originator of some few specific principles that almost became an obsession with certain of his later colleagues, concerning the decoration of flat surfaces. His sense of logic wounded to the quick, he complained in his *True Principles* about certain forms of contemporary Gothic wallpapers,

> where a wretched caricature of a pointed building is repeated from the skirting to the cornice in glorious confusion,—door over pinnacle, and pinnacle over door.... Again, those papers which are shaded are defective in principle; for, as a paper is hung round a room, the ornament must frequently be shadowed on the light side.

Also,

> A moment's reflection must show the extreme absurdity of *repeating a perspective* over a large surface with some hundred different points of sight: a panel or wall may be enriched and decorated at pleasure, but it should always be treated in a consistent manner.... Flock papers [another variety of the species] are admirable substitutes for the ancient hangings, but then they must consist of pattern *without shadow,* with the forms relieved by the introduction of harmonious colours. .... These observations will apply to modern carpets, the patterns of which are generally *shaded.* Nothing can be more ridiculous than an apparently *reversed groining* to walk upon, or highly relieved foliage and perforated tracery for the decoration of a floor.
>
> The ancient paving tiles are quite consistent with their purpose, being merely ornamented with a pattern not produced by any apparent relief, but only by *contrast of colour;* and carpets should be treated in precisely the same manner.

In view of this, Turkey carpets "are by far the handsomest now manufactured". They "have no shadow in their pattern, but merely an intricate combination of coloured intersections".[17]

Another hobby-horse of later designers was the problem of how to treat natural form for ornamental purposes. This will be given a fuller treatment further on; Pugin was evidently no forerunner on this point, but even so, he found his way to the generally accepted principles all alone. In his last book on design, *Floriated Ornament,* published in 1849, he gave an account of how, at some time in the course of his studies, he

became fully convinced that the finest foliage work in the Gothic buildings were all close approximations to nature, and that their peculiar character was chiefly owing to the manner of their arrangement and disposition.

He refers here to Southwell and to the Sainte-Chapelle in Paris, and goes on:

The more carefully I examined the productions of the mediaeval artists, in glass painting, decorative sculpture, or metal work, the more fully I was convinced of their close adherence to natural forms .... It is absurd, therefore, to talk of *Gothic* foliage. The foliage is *natural*, and it is the *adaptation* and *disposition* of it which stamps the style. The great difference between antient and modern artists in their adaptation of nature for decorative purposes, is as follows. The former disposed the leaves and flowers of which their design was composed into geometrical forms and figures, carefully arranging the stems and component parts so as to *fill up* the space they were intended to enrich; and they were represented in such a manner as not to destroy the consistency of the peculiar feature or object they were employed to decorate, by merely imitative rotundity or shadow; for instance, a pannel, which by its very construction is flat, would be ornamented by leaves or flowers drawn out or extended, so as to display their geometrical forms on a flat surface.

An example of Pugin's own style in this respect is given in *Fig. 10*. The passage goes on:

On the other hand, a modern painter would endeavour to give a fictitious idea of relief, as if *bunches* of flowers were laid on, and, by dint of shadow and foreshortening, an appearance of cavity or projection would be produced on a feature which architectural consistency would require to be treated as a plane.[18]

The quotation calls for no comment other than an excuse for its length, which must pass in view of the great prominence of this principle in the theory of design after Pugin.

Besides these more general principles, Pugin has an odd comment here and there which throws light on his attitude to the everyday aspects of his profession. Thus, to take an instance, he railed like William Morris against "modern upholstery", which is made a surprising vehicle for bad and paltry taste .... in the case of curtains, ... the modern plans of suspending enormous folds of stuff over poles, as if for the purpose of sale or of being dried, is quite contrary to the use and intentions of curtains, and abominable in taste ....

they also form "the depositories of thick layers of dust, and in London not unfrequently become the strong-holds of vermin."

Pugin's work as a designer and a producer of design offers several interesting traits. He seems to be the first of that well-known type of Victorian artist who, unable to find satisfying objects for furnishing and decoration in the open market, set up workshops to produce them himself. Like Morris, Pugin built a house—or rather, in succession, two houses—for himself, both of them in unplastered red brick—also like Morris's *Red House* which Philip Webb built for him in 1859. Like Morris, too, he furnished his home with furniture, etc. of his own design, and designed clothes and jewellery for his wife.[19]

His workshop—for which his youthful attempt to produce Gothic ornament on a commercial basis was only an unsuccessful precursor—was lodged eventually in his home, *The Grange* at Ramsgate, south-east of London. The house, still standing, is in itself of considerable interest, including a chapel for private service, on the furnishing and upkeep of which Pugin spent large sums. At Ramsgate he kept a corps of assistants, who prepared, under his strict supervision, many of the designs for his works in the decorative arts. John Hardman Powell, nephew of Pugin's great friend and business partner John Hardman of Birmingham, was the first to arrive, and except for a few short holidays he lived and worked at Ramsgate from 1845 until Pugin's death in 1852. By 1848, there appear to have been sometimes five or six men at work on the designs. One young man, Carolani, imported by Pugin from the studio of Overbeck, the German artist, spent his entire time on the painting of ecclesiastical banners and triptychs.[20] Pugin himself gives a picture of the rich variety of objects produced at the Grange in a letter he wrote to A.-N. Didron, and which was considered of sufficient importance to be printed in the *Bulletin Archéologique, publié par le Comité Historique des Arts et Monuments* in 1843.[21]

In this letter, which ranks as a highly important personal document, Pugin gave a very full description of his works and of the methods in which they were carried out at Ramsgate. In view of his apparent tendency to glorify his own work,[22] it might be held that the general tone of this letter is somewhat high-pitched; but, again, on consulting certain specimens exhibited at the Victoria and Albert Museum in 1952, it seems correct to assume that Pugin's account of his many-sided activities, and the ideals that directed them, cannot be very wide of the mark. Again, the picture seems to offer striking parallels to the activities of William Morris ten or twenty years later: the products turned out were of a similar character, the stress on old-fashioned modes of workmanship was the same—as was, incidentally, the falling short of this ideal, both men allowing a more or less considerable percentage of their designs to be executed by industrial firms. Little is known about Pugin's attitude to his workmen; Ferrey, his biographer, stated that they "loved him", while Mrs. Stanton on the whole gives the impression that he drove them rather hard. That he did not expect much from them in the idealistic way, is clear from a letter written in answer to Mr. C. Bruce Allen, who had approached him for advice, in 1852, on the establishment of a school for "art-workmen, and a museum of architectural casts". Pugin wrote that he wished them every success, but expected them to find

no end of difficulties. Workmen are a singular class, and from my experience of them, which is rather extensive, are generally incapable of taking a high view on these subjects—and ready at a moment to leave their instructors and benefactors for an extra sixpence a day for the first bidder that turns up. I have been all my life instructing men, while others profited by the result of my labours. In the present state of society, and the total absence of anything like the faith and religious feeling that actuated men in past ages, I believe it is impossible to do much good.[23]

The belief here asserted, when finally it came to be shared by Morris, turned him into a social reformer—as it had done Ruskin before him. It had made Pugin join the Catholic Church. Thus, the interpretation of this particular problem was the same with all three, in spite of the different solutions they chose.

It has been stated that Pugin sent designs to industrial firms for execution. As a matter of fact, before the full establishment of his workshop at Ramsgate, he had obtained connections with manufacturing firms who produced his designs in various materials. Prominent among these was Minton's, of Stoke-upon-Trent, who took care of his tiles and after numerous experiments was able to produce satisfactory wares.[24] His stained glass was made by John Hardman & Co., Birmingham.[25] George Myers of Myers & Wilson at Hull was his builder from 1839 onward. Edward Hull of Wardour Street supplied him with valuable antiques, etc., and with textiles. By 1840,

he turned to a Mr. Tyler of London, who produced from his designs the vestments which he created to furnish the churches he designed. .... Hardman's sale of Pugin-designed goods was considerable and varied—iron and brass work, jewellery, book-clasps, etc., 1837—40.

Conspicuous among the jewellery were the pieces originally designed for his fiancée in 1843 and exhibited in the Gothic court of the Great Exhibition, where they were much admired by Queen Victoria. So, at least in the earlier stages of his career, Pugin was more a designer of art-manufactures than an architect; indeed, "not until his appointment, in April 1837, as the Architect of Scarisbrick Hall did his private practice as an architect truly begin."[26] He was a many-sided designer, including among his work most articles of furnishing and interior decoration, besides a great variety of ecclesiastical vestments and *objets d'art*. In this respect he differs from Morris, who was eminent only as a designer of flat pattern—that is wallpapers and textiles.

In yet another respect did the two men differ seriously in their attitude, namely to modern convenience of mechanical invention, and to modern means of mechanical machine production and factory labour. Thus, while Morris hated railways and could easily picture himself traversing the country on the hindquarters of a donkey,

Pugin saw in them "a fine scope for grand massive architecture", and produced an engraving showing an appropriate design for "Railway bridges on the antient principles *(Fig. 11)*, ... building exactly what was wanted in the simplest and most substantial manner,—mere construction."[27] Quite evidently, Morris's delight in the "unspoilt" countryside, its character dominated by rural agricultural life, was not entirely shared by Pugin. Similarly, Ruskin's conception, shared by Morris, of mechanical aids to labour being objectionable on what we can only call moral grounds, would not have held water with Pugin, who contended that

in matters purely mechanical, the Christian architect should gladly avail himself of those improvements and increased facilities that are suggested from time to time. The steam engine is a most valuable power for sawing, raising, and cleansing stone, timber, and other materials.

Ruskin's views on this matter will be brought to light later; he believed that the artistic impulse was conveyed through the hand only; and even where the work did not demand any great share of it, he seems to have thought that any but the simplest forms of mechanical aid robbed the worker of his creative pleasure by killing his imaginative faculties. These were views which Pugin only partly endorsed. By "saving and expedition" in the *mechanical* part of building he wanted to save funds and manual labour "to expend on enrichments and variety of detail".[28] With regard to the execution of the latter, Pugin on the one hand and Ruskin and Morris on the other seem to hold similar views, and Pugin objected to

Putty pressing, plaster and iron casting for ornaments, wood burning, etc. .... *on account of their being opposed in their very nature to the true principles of art and design,*—by substituting monotonous repetitions for beautiful variety, flatness of execution for bold relief, encouraging cheap and false magnificence, and reducing the varied principles of ornamental design, which should be in strict accordance with the various buildings and purposes in which it is used, to a mere ready-made manufacture. But while, on the one hand, we should utterly reject the use of castings as substitutes for ornamental sculpture, we should eagerly avail ourselves of the great improvements in the working of metals for constructive purposes.

The general principle Pugin summed up as follows:

We do not want to arrest the course of inventions, but to confine these inventions to their legitimate uses, and to prevent their substitution for nobler arts.

But in his consideration of this problem, Pugin was exclusively concerned with the work of art. Unlike Ruskin and Morris he was not convinced of the destructive effect of mechanical labour on the operative nor did he care about it; he relegated to the machine such work as could easily do without the subtler touch of the human hand. In this respect, he was probably by far the most up-to-date of the three. In fact—as in the case of the railway—he was quite prepared to accept new technical devices calculated to ease the material side of life, writing that

Any modern invention which conduces to comfort, cleanliness, or durability, should be adopted by the consistent architect .. There is no reason in the world why noble cities, combining all possible convenience of drainage, water-courses, and conveyance of gas, may not be erected in the most consistent and yet Christian character [meaning, of course, Gothic]. *Every building that is treated naturally, without disguise or concealment, cannot fail to look well.*

It was indeed a combination of ancient spirit and contemporary form for which Pugin was pleading, when writing that *"it is the devotion, majesty, and repose of Christian art, for which we are contending;—it is not a style, but a principle."*

So Pugin acknowledged contemporary material progress; and the modern reader cannot help being puzzled at his position between the two—as it seems to us—contrasting forces of love for a style of the past on the one hand, and what can only be called the principle of modern functionalism, on the other. He was, as we have just seen, no advocate of stylistic copyism. It was the *principle* of the old style he was after, and therefore he wanted architects who were not

mere servile imitators of former excellence of any kind, but men imbued with the consistent spirit of the ancient architects, who would work on their principles, and carry them out as the old men would have done, had they been placed in similar circumstances, and with similar wants to ourselves.

Obviously, he wanted—or at least expected—architecture to deve-lop; and from the very nature of development he may somehow have seen that he would not be able to predict where it would lead, and that it might not always be kept within the trammels of a Gothic-like form—not even a Gothic enriched with gas and water pipes and still further conveniences which he could not foresee. However, his love—or prejudice—for Gothic was sufficiently strong at the time to allow him to disregard this apparent conflict, and concentrate on the emotional side of the matter. His *Apology* was concluded with the following words:

The present revival of ancient architecture in this country . . . . [besides being] . . . . warranted by religion, government, climate, and the wants of society, . . . is a perfect expression of all we should hold sacred, honourable, and national, and connected with the holiest and dearest associations.

This was written in 1843.

The amazing fact is that at that date Pugin was only 31 years old, and in spite of his being already a very famous architect with a long and extensive practice behind him, it is absurd to believe that the last word of a great man has been said at that age—if his activity is not somehow cut short. Naturally enough, Pugin was conscious of a personal development going on with regard to his own work; when he published his *Principles* in 1841, he wrote sensibly enough that "Christian verity" compelled him

to acknowledge that there are hardly any defects which I have pointed out to you in the course of this Lecture which could not with propriety be illustrated by my own productions at some period of my professional career. Truth is only gradually developed in the mind, and is the result of long experience and deep investigation.[29]

It is hardly too daring to suggest that during the last eleven years of his life, increasing experience and further investigation might have brought him to a point where he found himself compelled to resolve what to a modern critic seems so very much like an inconsistency between the modernity of his theories, and the retro-

37

spective character of his work. His latest critic, Mrs. Phoebe Stanton, indeed more than suggests such a development; in her own words,

he was an artist who perceived beyond the stylistic limitations he imposed on himself principles of design and spatial aesthetic possibilities. Had he not died so young there is little doubt but that he would have spent his capacities upon the latter of these roles, for he had, in spite of his human misery and illness, spent his last years upon the solving of this dilemma ... By the end of his short life he had come to realise that his adherence to authorities was futile. He may well have stood at the brink of discovery when in 1851 he summarised his own career in these words in a letter to John Hardman:

"My writings, much more than what I have been able to do, have revolutionised the taste of England. My cause as an architect is run out.... I am really ashamed of our things.... Our things are only good when compared with the Beasts, the Brutes, who belong to this age, but by the true standard they make me ill. As we gain knowledge conviction of failure is inevitable .... Dear me, a few years ago I felt quite satisfied with things we now look upon as abominable. Still I almost sigh for old simplicity when I thought all the old cathedral men fine fellows. It is all delusion." [30]

At least this letter proves a strong dissatisfaction with his own work; but it gives little or no clue as to what his next step would have been, had he been able to work on. Would he have continued a Gothic architect? Or would he have beaten a completely new track, creating startling innovations?

Much as one may regret to say so, it is doubtful if he would; at least he showed no high appreciation of the one spectacular building of his age, which was hailed by many as the precursor of an architecture which was to embody a new conception of beauty: being asked by Paxton what he thought of his Crystal Palace, he retorted—"Think, ... why, that you had better keep to building greenhouses, and I will keep to my churches and cathedrals." According to Ferrey, "He could see no evidence of artistic treatment in its composition, and railed vehemently against the style of ornament employed." Besides, cast-iron pillars "were odious things in his sight." [31]

In the face of this attitude of Pugin's, it would be rash to draw absolute conclusions on the point of his further development—an irrelevant matter anyhow, since his career was cut off by premature death in 1852. His great and indisputable achievement rests therefore on his writings, as he himself realised. The body of ideas set forth in them was deduced by Pugin from one particular style, and he applied them to recreate this style in his own time. In their phrasing, however, many among his principles are of such general soundness and common sense that they could stimulate artists of the most diverse creeds; hence Pugin's outstanding position among the theorists of the Victorian age.

Part I: 1835–1851

PARLIAMENTARY REPORTS
AND THE REFORM GROUP

1836 was the important year when Pugin the younger established himself in the public consciousness as a man with much to say on the decorative arts—and one who was liable to say it. But the thing was in the air: with the building of the British Museum begun in 1828, and the competition for the new Houses of Parliament, the times were pregnant with official interest in the arts; out of this a Parliamentary Committee was born, "to inquire into the best means of extending a knowledge of the arts and of the principles of design among the people (especially the manufacturing population) of the country."[1] This happened in 1835. The Committee continued well into the next year, and a long list of manufacturers, artists, and men otherwise considered competent to give their views, were examined before it.[2] The main questions with which the examiners occupied themselves were the inferiority of English products as compared with, for example, French work; enquiries into the comparative state of art-education at home and abroad; and the extent to which England depended on piracy of foreign designs and models. In this last connection, it should be remembered that before 1839 patent laws for the protection of *designs* as distinct from inventions only existed for designs printed on textiles; but in this year Parliament passed "An Act to secure to Proprietors of Design for Articles of Manufacture the Copyright of such Designs for a limited Time."[3]

This Act gave a protection of three months to most designs, and for metal-work three years. It was probably of great help in England, but it may also have increased the dependence on foreign designs, because, as we learn from a contemporary observer,

Manchester was utterly dependent on France for designs for calico-prints, and spent £30,000 a year for them in the early forties. Similar conditions prevailed as regarded Spitalfields silks, Coventry ribbon, and Birmingham brass and bronze.[4]

The Parliamentary enquiry in 1835 was brought about by commercial and trade interests, to acquire information as to Britain's position in the world market; art and good design were estimated or not according as they increased demand and made the position of English goods stronger in competition with foreign ones. From now on we shall come up against new and practical considerations which lead away from the somewhat transcendent idealism which characterised Pugin's efforts in the higher and lower reaches of his art. For the next twenty years official and departmental forces become important sources of very interesting theories of art-manufacture and design.

With the Parliamentary Committee of 1835 we are at the beginning of things as far as official principles in our particular field are concerned, though the reports do not give much material. *James Nasmyth*, the inventor of the steam hammer, stressed the importance of "the entire reconcileability of elegance of form with bare utility," and said that examples of ancient art owed their beauty to "the employment of the smallest number of lines in giving form to the object in view." To the examiner's question that "There is probably no example of a perfect machine which is not at the same time beautiful?" *Thomas Leverton Donaldson*, architect and hon. secretary to the Institute of British Architects, answered, "I know none." *David Ramsay Hay*, interior decorator from Edinburgh, and author of a book on the *Laws of harmonious Colouring, adapted to Interior Decorations* (published 1828), recommended the study of natural forms, especially plants, to find inspiration for ornament and design in nature, "and thereby form a school peculiar to this country."⁵ These are statements interesting in themselves, but it is evident from the general context in which they appear that they were isolated utterances without any roots in a general and comprehensive system of ideas.

As a result of this Inquiry, a *Normal School of Design* was established at Somerset House in 1837, with several branches in manufacturing districts in the provinces, and courses were held in elementary drawing and in drawing as applied to various industries. Of practical instruction there was none according to the plan, although "it deserves special mention that in 1838 William Dyce, the English 'Nazarener', set up a loom in the school,"⁶ of which he was director from 1838–43. I have also come across some references to a kiln for pottery, and a potter's wheel;⁷ but these were the symbols of a want rather than the manifestations of an established reality, and in fact the schools remained little more than elementary drawing classes. Such as they were, however, they mark the first effort to "marry art to industry", as it was then phrased, and they point to a feeling of educational responsibility on the part of the State in these matters.

The arrangement was not a success. The administration of the schools was rendered ineffective through being placed in the hands of a large, unpaid board, consisting mainly of Academy painters and dilettanti of various kinds, all of whom were very irregular attendants at board meetings. In the schools, work was impeded by lack of understanding on the part of manufacturers, in some cases, and more generally by lack of agreement as to the lines along which teaching was to be directed. But in spite of all this, 16 branches had been established by 1849, and, most probably, the schools had at least done a great deal to raise the standard of drawing among workmen. However, new parliamentary committees set up in 1847 and 1849, condemned the whole scheme as " 'An utter and complete failure'. Nothing, the Committee said, was done at the school but copying of drawings. Industry, now as before, employed only a few designers."⁸ However, the last of these Reports forms far more rewarding reading than the one from 1835—36. Among the witnesses were men who for shorter or longer periods had been in contact with the recent Schools of Design, either as teachers or otherwise, and others who had formed more or less definite views on the theoretical side of the matter. Among the 39 witnesses therefore we meet persons who are of the highest importance for the present examination. The sculptor *John Bell*, who had been Visitor of the school for several years and had taken over temporarily the duties of headmaster in 1849; *Henry Cole*, later Sir Henry and a K. C. B., but at the time an energetic civil servant of long standing; although perhaps something of a busy-body, he had shown himself on various occasions to be an efficient organiser. His claims to authority in artistic matters rested with his publication of popular guide books on historic monuments, and with his position as an organiser of a kind of firm for the production of Art-Manufactures; indeed, it is even possible that he coined the phrase himself.[9] His connection with the Schools of Design, slight as it was, dated from 1839, when his preoccupation with wood-engraving had turned his attention towards it;[10] in 1847 he was asked by the then Secretary of the Board of Trade to lecture at the school, which honour he declined; instead, being a man who was never afraid of causing a stir, he wrote three Reports to the Board—also on the instigation of the Secretary—on the state of affairs in the school, making some very apt suggestions for improvements, largely on the organising side. Cole's Reports were written in 1848, and to some extent they were responsible for the enquiry of the following year.

Among the witnesses was also *William Dyce*, R.A., whom we have already had occasion to mention. Apart from his directorship between 1839 and 1843, he also acted at times as treasurer, as secretary to the council of the schools, inspector of provincial schools, and as master of the class for ornament between 1847 and 1848, when he resigned because of his disagreement with the system of teaching. With his Jacquard loom and his potter's wheel Dyce was decidedly one of, if not even *the* most prominent *avant-gardiste* within the school, even if his experiment had to be abandoned because of the

43

insufficient pre-education of the students—and probably because of some other difficulties as well.

Of other painters there were *Richard Redgrave*, A.R.A., who was appointed master of the class of colour; *George Wallis*, in charge of Spitalfields School of Design in 1843 and headmaster of the Manchester school from 1844–46, was the only one among them who had received his full training in the Schools. Then there was also the architect *Matthew Digby Wyatt*, later to become first Slade Professor at Cambridge. To these men, and a very few more, we shall have to turn for the development of theory in the 'forties and 'fifties.

The Report of 1849 makes it clear that the theorists within the Schools of Design had so far been separated into two main camps. In one were those who thought that imitative drawing was sufficient training for any designer; in the other were grouped those who felt that design was separated from pictorial art of a representational nature, being a different form of art altogether, with separate principles. They wanted to give practical instruction in the technical production of design, and insisted on some kind of formal modification of it to suit the material and technique for which it was made, as well as the various particular conditions under which the article would be used. They believed, in other words, that the designer perforce had to deviate from imitative representation in order to reach the compromise of a design satisfying from all artistic, technical, and utilitarian points of view; and they tried to find a set of rules to guide the artist who worked under the necessity of this compromise.

Prominent within this latter group, William Dyce had experimented with his loom and his potter's wheel, and had also been the first of a new school of thought. In 1842–43 he edited a *Drawing-book of the School of Design*,[11] and wrote a short Preface to it; this marked the starting point for the new line of speculation on the theoretical side of design, and provides an interesting parallel to

Pugin's almost contemporary principles of ornamental treatment. For the first time in the history of the Schools of Design Dyce set out in print the principle that design involved something besides and beyond mere imitative drawing.

Neither Pugin nor Dyce wanted to do away with ornament in objects of everyday use; the Victorian love of decoration, and plenty of it at that, was by no means a passion unknown to most of the reformers—as for the sake of convenience we may call them.

Indeed, their aim might be said to have been a reform of the art of ornamentation more than of design, since their chief energy was directed towards the perfect execution of existing forms of ornament, as well as towards finding new ones which were not to come under the heads either of stylistic copyism or of accurate and close imitation from forms in nature. They ascribed the highest importance to ornament as such, and their criticism of contemporary commercial design was largely directed against fallacies in the application of it—such as mixing of styles, or the use of a kind of ornament inappropriate to its place, or the more general sin of inartistic and ugly execution of ornamental detail, with other matters of this kind.

Before the Parliamentary Committee of 1836, D. R. Hay had pointed out the necessity of reverting to a study of natural forms to "form a school peculiar to this country".[12] Dyce's *Drawing-book* is concerned with the problems arising out of such a study, and out of the study of historic styles in decorative art.

The true end of all design is the attainment of beauty, and "There is no one who doubts that nature must be held up as the source from whence, as much now as ever, all the forms of beauty applicable to the uses of the ornamentist must be derived." But nature must not be studied for a close copyism of forms, but rather to learn "the contrivances by which she has adorned her works"; and thus, "ornamental art is rather *abstractive* and *reproductive* than imitative." In order to attain to "a new style of ornament" by inspiration from nature, Dyce held it desirable to go to the well-established authorities of ancient art, because they "may be proved to be founded on the most accurate perception of the *objective* causes of natural beauty—because, in short, they are facts and conclusions already arrived at." Dyce's own conclusion is that the designer must "anatomise" the works of nature, and that

the power of representing objects in the form of diagrams is to him far more necessary and valuable than that of imitating them with all their effects of light and shade, of surface or of material, as an artist does. This acquirement, therefore, of drawing with precision and readiness every variety of superficial form in outline . . . . must be a prominent object in the education of ornamentists,

whose education "can neither be ranked under the head of artistical imitation, nor of practical geometry", but should lie somewhere between the two. This talk of "diagrams" and of representing natural form in outline links up very well with Pugin's contemporary insistence on a flat treatment of forms borrowed from nature when applied to objects like wallpapers and tiles. Both writers justified their principles by referring to practice in ancient art—Dyce, in a general way, Pugin, of course, with specific reference to Gothic. In recommending nature as the basis of all ornamental design, however, Dyce is seven years ahead of his great contemporary.

Dyce must have been one of several who occupied themselves with similar investigations into the laws of design, even if few of them are known to us in print. The problem of formal treatment of ornament was, for instance, taken up by D.R. Hay when he published a book on *Original geometrical Diaper Designs, accompanied by An Attempt to develope and elucidate the true Principles of Ornamental Design, as applied to the Decorative Arts*, in 1844. He wanted to emulate "the principles of combinations which constitute beauty", so as to enable the designer to "produce it in his work", and insisted on flatness of design and conventional treatment of ornament—but he contributed nothing essentially new.

So, little or nothing of interest was written for some years after Dyce had formulated his basic suggestions for further efforts in the Schools of Design, and the next important step was of a more practical nature and was connected with the name of Henry Cole. He was, as we know, an interested amateur, and had even written some articles in the *Athenaeum* about "Decoration",[13] where the references to the literature of the subject include the writings of D.R.Hay, Goethe and Eastlake. His handbooks on historic monuments began to appear in 1841, under the *nom de plume* of Felix Summerly,[14] and went on for eight years. Then, in 1846, this many-sided civil servant actually designed and produced, as it seems almost with his own hands, a tea-set for which he won a prize at an exhibition arranged in London by the Society of Arts *(Fig. 12)*. Cole's way of setting about this feat is typical of the entire movement to which he was later to belong: he went to the British Museum to consult "Greek earthenware for authority for handles", thus showing his veneration for an acknowledged authority of the past—not copying but seeking inspiration in a most commendable manner. Then he went in person to the Minton works at Stoke-on-Trent, where "he passed three days in superintending the throwing, turning, modelling, and moulding" of the tea-set.[15] Considerable thought was given to fit form to function. The milk jug, for instance,

has three lips like some articles of Etruscan Pottery, enabling the liquid to be poured at both angles, right and left, which requires only a motion of the wrist, whilst the usual method needs lifting of the arm. .... The plate is smaller than usual in the rim, because much size in that part is needless.

Cole's tea-set was an effort to demonstrate that "elegant forms may be made not to cost more than inelegant ones," and provides a very good example of a radical designer's attempt to unite use and beauty with low cost. Thus, the relative simplicity of the design was not the result of any idealism in that respect on Cole's part: he was as ornamental in his taste as everybody else at that time, and used the expressions "beauty" and "ornament" almost as synonyms when writing that "the aim in these models has been to obtain as much beauty and ornament as is commensurate with cheapness. A higher standard in the ornamental parts would have led to much greater cost."[16] The tea-set was a great commercial success and spurred Cole

47

on to start a kind of organisation to create an alliance between fine art and manufactures, which he hoped "would promote public taste".[17] This was *Summerly's Art-Manufactures*, started in 1847.

This interesting enterprise formed an industrial counterpart to Pugin's attempts to produce objects for contemporary use in a mediaeval manner. Cole's efforts were wholly directed towards improving contemporary industrial products, and there is no high idealism about the enterprise in the manner of Pugin and Ruskin. He enlisted a great number of painters and sculptors, mostly academicians, including well-known names like that of *Sir R. Westmacott*, and several artists connected with the Schools of Design were appointed as teachers, *C. Horsley, R. Redgrave* and *H. J. Townsend* being the most prominent ones.[18] Together they brought into the Summerly products that strong love for story-telling which was so significant in painting and sculpture at that day; John Bell, the sculptor, designed "A Bride's Inkstand", with a little darling honeymoon Cupid carrying quills in his quiver, while supporting an upright taper in his right hand. Redgrave was the author of "The 'Well Spring', a Water Vase or Jug, in glass . . . . The ornament is of water plants coloured and enamelled on the glass, with gilt handles",[19] etc., etc. The whole tendency was very aptly described by a contemporary as "intimate uniting of high art and ornament, or what might be called in these days of new verbal coinage, the *Cellinesque*".[20] It must, of course, be understood that objects were only designed, not executed by Cole's artistic associates. At a time when the reputation of Britain's most gifted sculptor must have suffered through his association with the "low" art of designing for the hardware trade,[21] it was in itself a remarkable achievement to enlist any great number of "high" artists for similar purposes. The whole enterprise is very reminiscent of the days of Josiah Wedgwood, when George Adams, architect to the King, did not feel superior to applying his art to the potter's craft, and when the Staffordshire manufactures benefited from the genius of a Flaxman; this kind of practice seems to have become obsolete in Victorian times with the increasing gulf

separating workman and artist. That period's extraordinary veneration for the "high" arts of sculpture, painting, and architecture, is
reflected, as much as in anything else, in the pictorial artist's almost
total neglect of designing for objects of everyday use. It is therefore significant in this respect, that the Summerly pamphlet opens
with a reminder of the days of old in which the artist also lent his
power to the enriching of humbler everyday life; names like those
of Giotto, Leonardo, Holbein, and Reynolds are quoted in support.

In the pamphlet, the purpose of the Summerly enterprise is
clearly summed up: the basic idea was to revive "the good old
practice of connecting the best Art with familiar objects in
daily use". In spite of the "Cellinesque" tendencies of the group,
"superior utility . . . . is not to be sacrificed to ornament." Logic
must direct the application of ornament, so that each object would
be decorated "with appropriate details relating to its use"; and ornamental detail should be obtained "as directly as possible from
Nature". The sum total of all this was a style insisting upon a lavish
use of judiciously applied naturalistic ornament on objects of everyday use, and *Summerly's Art-Manufactures* represented an attempt
at purifying the existing Mid-Victorian decorative style. Insisting
on naturalism it followed the trend of the day, but ran counter to a
growing understanding of formal treatment of pattern as advocated
by Dyce; but the insistence upon "superior utility", and the fact
that the Summerly artists discarded stylistic copyism and adaptation, choosing instead the equally Victorian but more promising
road of inspiration from nature—these two factors somewhat justify
the hope expressed in the Advertising Pamphlet that the Summerly
products might "possibly contain the germs of a style which England of the nineteenth century may call its own."

But Cole was also connected with another venture, maybe of
higher significance; this was a neat little monthly called the *Journal
of Design and Manufacture*, which began to appear in 1849 under
the editorship either of Redgrave or Cole.[22]

The journal was a small review of design and manufacture, with

49

engraved and woodcut illustrations, and included samples of wall-papers and various materials. It was backed by the same group of men who are by now familiar from the Schools of Design and from *Summerly's Art-Manufactures*—names like George Wallis, J. C. Horsley, R. Redgrave, W. Dyce, M. D. Wyatt, and John Bell, to-gether with the German exile *Gottfried Semper*, architect of the Dresden Opera House, and his British colleague *Owen Jones*. Jones had published *Plans, Elevations, Sections and Details of the Alhambra* (in 1836 and 1842—45), with other books on art; he went on adding to the list until his death in 1874. The *Journal of Design* became the mouthpiece of these men, and in it appeared the first important written contributions to principles of design since the publication of Dyce's drawing-book six years earlier.

Indeed, the *Journal* was acutely aware of the need for principles in its field, and maintained from the very start "something like a systematic attempt to establish recognized principles"; part of their aim was, in this respect, "to fortify all our more important crit-icims .... at least with the reasons on which they were based."[23]

In their theoretical outlook the writers of the *Journal* were, many of them, strongly influenced by the non-religious and non-mediae-val side of Pugin's writings. The *Journal* held that he "deserves all the respect which is due to an artist who has adopted principles to guide him, and who manfully maintains them and carries them into practice." Writing on ironwork, Digby Wyatt owned that

After the admirable remarks made by Mr. Pugin, in his "True Principles of Christian Architecture", any observations we could offer upon our subject, in connexion with Gothic architecture, would but be superfluous; yet we cannot refrain from bearing a humble tribute to the truth and justice of many of his propositions.[24]

Similarly, in subsequent years laudatory references to him are found in most of the important writings on design emanating from this circle.

Like *Summerly's Art-Manufactures*, the *Journal of Design* worked mainly to improve standards within the accepted order of things.

It was edited in a commercial spirit, and its criticism was adapted to the standards and needs of a well-to-do middle class. In the introductory address to the first volume the "*moral* influence of ornamental art" is said to extend "to millions"; but whereas no further explanation is offered on this point, it is strongly affirmed that "the *commercial* value of ornamental design now comes home practically to the perception of tens of thousands,—to manufacturers, artists, and designers; to artisans and dealers in decorative manufactures;" whereupon many a good example is given to prove this proposition and to show how a little artistic embellishment on some useful article has increased its sale and rolled pounds into the pockets of its manufacturer. In full keeping with this the *Journal* intended to be "thoroughly conservative of the best interests of manufacturers, designers, and all parties concerned"—some of its pet hobby-horses being "better laws and a better tribunal to protect copyright in designs, and . . . . a largely increased extension of copyright". It also declared that it meant to "wage war against all pirates [of design]". It wanted to reform the Schools of Design, to make them "business-like realities", and declared itself at enmity with fashion, because "the restless demands of the public for constant novelty are alike mischievous to the progress of good ornamental art as they are to all commercial interests."[25]

In addition to its samples and its criticisms, the *Journal* published "Original Papers" on "Copyright in Design", warnings against "Mixtures of Styles", book reviews, an article on the "History of the constitution of the 'Government' school of design and its proceedings," a "Lecture on Ornament delivered to the Students of the London School of Design", "Table Talk", and "Correspondence"— all in the first issue; and the succeeding ones are of a similar character. Scattered throughout the six small volumes which contain all the issues of the *Journal* during its three years of existence, we find remarks of a dogmatic character that go far to suggest a comprehensive theory of form, sentiment, and conditions of production in design and applied art. The "Original Papers" were either specially

51

written for the *Journal*, or reprinted there largely from speeches or addresses given on subjects lying within its sphere of activities; occasionally extracts from odd newspaper articles also found their way to its pages. All this material may safely be quoted as harmonising with the *Journal's* general editorial outlook.

This outlook was very much marked by the general optimism which seemed to prevail in most fields of human activity with regard to the results and methods of science. It seems a safe assertion that at no time have the makers of rules in design been more convinced of their value; this was because the principles which by their superior human reason they had conceived, appeared to them to bear the hallmark of scientific truth. In his "Lecture on Ornament delivered to the Students of the London School of Design", as printed in the *Journal of Design*,[26] Dyce puts it like this: "Ornamental design is, in fact, a kind of practical science, which, like other kinds, investigates the phenomena of nature for the purpose of applying natural principles and results to some new end." That end was "the completeness of the results of mechanical skill". Such a statement implies a rationalistic, scientific attitude to a problem which is largely artistic; but this approach to aesthetics was probably as characteristic of the day as is the psychological one of our own. The basic justification for design, however, was grounded on something we may probably call a psychological necessity: it is necessary "because we all feel it to be so. The love of ornament is a tendency of our being . . . . ornamental design has had its birth long before the very conception of the fine arts."

The principles which Dyce set forth in his lecture are very much in keeping with his earlier practice at the Schools of Design. As a general rule, ornament should be "suited to particular *uses, situations, or fabrics*", and considered "with reference to the process by which a design is to be executed"; it is "of course, essential that the ornamentist should be perfectly conversant with the capabilities of the process." The end of this particular study was "to produce models and patterns which are workable, and to ascertain what amount of beautiful art the process is capable of reproducing". His more particular rules are strongly marked by his rationalistic attitude; he took up Pugin's principle of "uniform flatness and solidity" in floor patterns like carpets and mosaics—best conveyed through "designs geometrically constructed and capable of repetition". A natural precedent to this last feature was found in the repetition of crystalline forms. This, by the way, must be the first time we meet the shadow of Ruskin on the scene: his *Modern Painters* started to appear in 1843, and is full of this kind of justification of aesthetic features through imagined parallels of form in nature. But he will be discussed later.

However, Dyce was no doctrinaire believing in flat pattern at all costs. His reason told him that walls must be treated so as to retain the impression of constructive strength, whereas panels, if such there are, "may all be treated as if they were vacuities; that is to say, as so many openings into other rooms, into the street, or to the sky."[27] Here, "artistic imitation" and "full relief", with "landscapes, historical subjects, pictures of flowers, ornamental trelliswork" were entirely in their place, "since, in point of fact, the space may be treated precisely as the canvass is treated by the artist, that is to say, as a vacuity." On the strength of this, he at once dismissed

the crude and hazy notion that, *as a general rule*, flowers and all other objects must undergo a *conventionalising* process before they can be employed as matter of ornament. I at once get rid of any attempt to define generally the extent to which truth of resemblance to natural objects is admissible in ornament. There is no general rule. Each case must be considered by itself.

Ruskin would doubtless have supported this, writing, as he did later in *The Two Paths*, that "the greatest decorative art is wholly unconventional—downright, pure, good painting and sculpture."[28] Years later, Digby Wyatt also gave him support, writing that

the tendency of the chief directors of taste has been, as it appears to the author, to tie the decorative artist's hands somewhat too dogmatically. The result will be that .... our productions will grow dry and arid.[29]

At the end of his lecture, Dyce pleads again, as he did six years earlier, for the study of ancient art as "a storehouse, of which the treasures must be known by us before we are in a condition to become explorers in our turn."

The designer's attitude to nature had been made the subject of speculation by Dyce in his drawing-book, and also been referred to in his "Lecture on Ornament". The subject was one which attracted much attention among the pioneers. We know how Pugin had worked out an answer by himself, and we shall see how Ruskin made it a philosophical question of high moral import. Among the men in Henry Cole's circle, Richard Redgrave also gave his contribution in a lecture given in 1849 at the School of Design, afterwards printed in the *Journal*.[30] With him, as with others, application of ornament was the obvious method for the artistic embellishment of objects, and nature offered to him the equally obvious source of ornamental form, to the absolute exclusion of that stylistic copyism so dear to contemporary commercial designers. Redgrave insisted on "subjecting plants and flowers to a decorative or ornamental treatment, by a systematic combination and arrangement." Unlike Dyce, he must have regarded this as an absolute rule, since "It may be questioned whether, in any case, mere imitation can properly be called ornament." But as a means of study he advocated proceeding "by careful and even laboured imitation" to make the student "master thoroughly all the details of nature, and acquaint himself with the anatomy of her structure."

Nature, used as a source of ornament, also gave ample room for storytelling and sentiment, since Redgrave advocated that the designer choose for his ornaments such flowers or plants as appealed "to the knowledge and sympathies of those whom it is intended to please". He

must be able to link those stores of knowledge in some living relation to the thoughts of the poet, deeds of the hero, the patriot, or the martyr, or even to that humbler love, which in the popular mind, as shewn in the names of plants and flowers, clings to a connexion between sensible things and graceful or beautiful thoughts.

Thus, certainly, "The Greek who first so beautifully symbolised ‚ in the wave ornament the 'multitudinous sea', no doubt applied it in some temple to his maritime gods." Clearly, there must be logic in all things.

The actual artistic process by which natural form should be "reduced to ornament" was described by an anonymous writer in the *Journal:* it would be brought about

first by the selection of the most graceful forms, the few from amongst the many; then by the simplification of the parts, the seeing the general in the individual; then, if for a flat surface, by a certain amount of geometrical reduction to one surface, the absolute truth of form being in some degree merged in that which shall give the fullest impression of it. Moreover, if colour is to be added, this also must be simplified, the minor shades left out, the large masses retained. Then comes the consideration of the material, its glossiness or absorbent qualities, its open or close texture; and when we add to this the due consideration of the modes of manufacture, there is quite enough to engage the best attention of the designer honestly on his own fabric.[31]

By this time the theory of natural inspiration for design was complete; it involved two main principles, both of them fully understood: the *adaptation of form* and the *transportation of sentiment*. It became from now on part of the stock-in-trade of Victorian designers. One of the greater among them, Lewis F. Day, could add nothing essential to it when he wrote his *Nature in Ornament* in 1892. As this book has been re-edited and published in successive editions up to our own generation, we owe to the early Victorians the establishment of at least this one principle of lasting importance.

Besides this preoccupation with broad principles, the *Journal* bears witness to the lively discussion which must have been going on among those connected with it; small grains of theoretic wisdom are found scattered about its pages—for instance, the view that light materials ought to be decorated with a light design, or an editorial "objection on principle to the translation of the *woven* Cachmere effects to printing". Flatness is advocated for wallpaper design, and ornament must be subordinated to the character of the object for which it is intended. With few exceptions, the disapproval of false pretence, imitations, and shams, in their material and formal manifestations alike, is general, "from the stucco abomination, that, outfacing honest brick, affects to look like stone on the outside of our houses, to the thousand other shams which meet us within doors."[32] The *Journal of Design* felt a "wide vocation" to combat this and other errors. In Owen Jones's words, it realised that "the great industrial movement . . . arrived before the artistic world was prepared to acknowledge it"; it felt that "the new materials used, the new wants to be supplied, should and might have suggested forms more in harmony with the end in view."[33] Realising this, the men behind the *Journal* conscientiously sought to find these forms; their degree of failure or success must be measured against the vastness of the enterprise.

Part II: 1 8 5 1

CRITICISM BY PRINCIPLE

To our circle of reformers, striving to improve standards in industrial design, the Great Exhibition must in several respects have been a disappointment, and yet they had been instrumental in bringing it into being.

The Exhibition grew out of the activities of the Society of Arts, under the protection of Prince Albert, who had been its President since 1845. It was at one of the society's annual exhibitions that Henry Cole won a silver medal for his tea-set, and he became a member the same year—in 1846. Cole was a man who set things going wherever he appeared, and it was largely due to him that in 1851 the Society's exhibition grew into something quite without precedent—the first World Exhibition.

He brought with him his circle of fellow-workers from the Schools of Design, from Summerly's Art-Manufactures, and from the *Journal of Design*, and he added the German architect Gottfried Semper to the group. To quote Pevsner on this point—

These men whose views of the Exhibition coincided in so many ways, formed quite clearly a circle of friends and fellow-fighters in the cause of design. They were all in their thirties and forties at the time of the Exhibition .... and they appeared prominently at the Exhibition in one function or another. Semper designed the Canadian, Danish, Egyptian and Swedish displays, Owen Jones the colour-schemes of the whole structural parts of the interior—in primaries:

blue, yellow and red. Jones was also Superintendent of Class xxx, that is the class devoted to Sculpture etc., and of Class xvii, dealing with Paper, Printing etc. Wyatt was Secretary of the Executive Committee, and in addition responsible entirely for progress during the construction of the building. Dyce was a Juror for the iron and hardware class and a member of the prize-giving committee, Redgrave and Townsend sat on the Committee on Manufactures. Redgrave was also on the Jury for Sculpture etc., and wrote.... the official *Supplementary Report on Design* to the Jurors.[34]

In addition to these, George Wallis was deputy for Textile Manufactures, and Pugin held the high position of organiser of the Mediaeval Court, which counts among the most important manifestations of the Gothic Revival in England. He was also a juror for Sculpture, Models, and Plastic Art, together with Redgrave and others. This is the first time that we find a personal contact existing between Pugin and the group of pioneers with whom we have now been concerned; and it was unhappily to come to an end with Pugin's death only the year after. But in spite of this, his ideas were a constant influence with them, and their writings and lectures at this time abound in praise of him. In this way his share in their various enterprises was great, even if personally he had no part in them, and probably in many cases would not have approved anyhow.

The Great Exhibition, where now these men worked together, was designed to give a picture of the actual state of development reached in the various industries; and the truly vast and varied display of all manner of goods evoked corresponding amazement and admiration—unqualified among the general public, coupled with serious reflection and even regret among the thoughtful few. Our pioneers must be understood to belong to the second class, and the *Supplementary Report on Design*,[35] written by Redgrave for the Commissioners of the Exhibition when it was over, may be taken to represent the feeling of them all. Also, apart from the previous Parliamentary Reports, this was the first splendid opportunity of introducing into an official document the principles for which this group of reformers had been contending for over a decade.

The Report opens with some remarks of a general character: "ornament," Redgrave writes, "is merely the decoration of a thing constructed," and "is thus necessarily limited, for, so defined, it cannot be other than secondary, and must not usurp a principal place." In the Exhibition, however, the general tendency is to "construct ornament" rather than "ornament construction". Thus, one is led

to admire those objects of absolute utility (the machines and utensils of various kinds), where use is so paramount that ornament is repudiated, and, fitness of purpose being the end sought, a noble simplicity is the result (p.708).

Similar observations were made by Gottfried Semper, and by an anonymous writer in *The Times*, who characteristically enough, qualified his statement by adding that

we do not for a moment contend that the unbending precision which produces such great results in the cases quoted [tools, cotton-machinery, and the Crystal Palace itself] would be equally applicable to the manufactured products made available for our every-day and domestic wants and comforts[36]

—which attitude was most probably shared by Redgrave himself, if we consider the objects which were favoured with his praise.

Redgrave's Report echoes the favourite views of the *Journal of Design*: ornament must suit the material and function of the object for which it is intended, and "ornament originally carved in stone" may not be "used for metal or for wood, or, worse still, for carpets or for dresses" (p. 709). Ancient art should be resorted to for study, not for copyism (p. 709), and nature should be treated as a source of inspiration, not of imitation—"the endeavour ought to be to seize the simplest expression of a thing rather than to imitate it" (p. 710). He rails against the dictatorship of fashion —what he calls "constant search after novelty, ... one of the sources of bad taste" (p. 710), and also deals a blow on behalf of the designer when complaining of the manufacturers' stupidity when they hide the name of their designer so as to keep for the firm what praise his works may obtain; when they pay him less than his due, and when they set aside his artistic judgement and mutilate his designs according to their own notions of what will sell (p. 711); all these complaints, incidentally, are equally relevant to-day, a hundred years later, as anybody will be aware who knows something about the work of the present Council of Industrial Design in London.

Then follow Redgrave's comments on the various classes of exhibits, in each case with a reference to the principles on which he based his judgement. His indebtedness to Pugin for some of his ideas is obvious and needs no comment. Of Pugin himself, Redgrave held the highest opinion, and always spoke of him and his work in laudatory terms.

Starting with wallpapers and similar materials to cover flat surfaces, we meet the usual insistence on flat, conventional treatment of ornament—not too obtrusive in its general effect, because the walls should serve in most cases only as a background for the furniture, etc., of a room. For floors as well, flatness must be retained as an essential part of their character, because

imitative treatments are objectionable on principle, both as intruding on the sense of flatness, and as being too *attractive* in their details and colour to be sufficiently retiring and unobtrusive.

It is also necessary

to advert to a perfectly different treatment of these materials quite at variance with these rules, and bound by no such principles, by which paper-hanging becomes a pseudo-decoration, the wall being divided into compartments often irrespective of architectural construction, and pilasters, friezes, and mouldings imitated in false relief on its surface, with compositions of pictures, statues, hangings, flowers, fruits, etc., skilfully designed and well drawn .... it is, however, at best but a sham decoration, amenable to no laws, necessarily false in light and shade, often constructively inapplicable, and always impertinent and obtrusive (p. 717).

Decoration must be logical to be good, and Redgrave is more strict in his application of logic in this particular respect than Dyce had been in his lecture of 1849. Reason also rules designs for carpets, where

flatness should be one of the principles for decorating a surface continually under the feet: therefore all architectural relief ornaments, and all *imitations* of fruit, shells, and other solid or hard substances, or even of flowers, strictly speaking, are the more improper the more imitatively they are rendered.

Violent contrasts of light and dark, or of colour, should not be found,

but graduated shades of the same colour, or a distribution of colours nearly equal in scale of light and dark, should be adopted; secondaries and tertiaries, or neutralized primaries, being used rather than pure tints, and lights introduced merely to give expression to the forms. Under such regulations as to flatness and contrast, either geometrical forms, or scrolls clothed with foliation in any style, leaves, flowers, or other ornament, may be used (p. 727).

In the Exhibition, Indian and Turkish carpets reach the highest degree of excellence as measured against these standards (p. 729).

Both Dyce and Hay had urged the importance of geometry as a basic element of design, and Redgrave considers it vital, "not necessary as a principle of art", but "essentially required as the basis of ornament", which has "a geometrical distribution, and is subject to symmetry and correspondence of parts". This was said in connection with Garment Fabrics, but the principle has wider application, because "it may be truly said that it is confounding these provinces, and a departure from this true foundation on the part of the ornamentist, that has caused so much bad ornament in the various manufactures of the Exhibition" (p. 743).

From geometry and flat-pattern designs we then turn to aesthetic values of design seen in their relation to qualities of material. An example may be found in glass, of which the most prominent features are "its brilliancy of surface and its transparency, both of which should ever be preserved with the greatest care in all right treatment of glass", and not be ground away "so as to render them perfectly opaque;" nor should colour be injuriously applied [so as] to destroy purity, and prevent a proper enjoyment of the glowing lustre of the liquid contents... Another excellence of glass is its lightness, as compared with its power of containing: the maintenance of this quality is opposed to the heavy and deep surface-cutting to which glass is now so frequently submitted (p. 735).

Similar reflections are made concerning pottery and china, and its decoration, where, in addition to insistence on flat and conventionalised decoration, the necessity for stylistic unity is also urged, to prevent "the imitation of the ornament peculiar to one age and one purpose on the utensils of another age, ... which are intended for totally different uses" (p. 734). The case for functional forms is most strongly put in dealing with furniture:

the first consideration of the designer should be *perfect adaptation to intended use;* this may appear so obvious a truism as to want no enforcement, but a walk through the Exhibition will speedily undeceive us, for there we see a multitude of objects offending against this rule. .... Manufacturers should also aim at obtaining the greatest amount of convenience and accommodation in the least space, in order that the furniture may be as suitable as possible to the size and uses of the apartment in which it is placed.—Another consideration to be attended to is stability of construction, *apparent* as well as *real*; the first being necessary to satisfy the eye, the last being indispensable to excellence and durability... The constructive forms, moreover, should not be obscured by the ornament, but rather brought out by it; .... Over-enrichment, indeed, destroys itself .... contrast is one of the finest elements of pleasure, and .... *repose* is one of the most valued excellences of art; thus simplicity serves as the background to ornament, as the setting to the gem (p. 720).

Similar observations present themselves with regard to porcelain, glass, and pottery, where

the purest forms should be sought, allied to the greatest convenience and capaciousness; and the requisite means of lifting, holding, supporting,—of filling, emptying, and cleansing, should engage the attention of the designer, before the subject of their ornamentation is at all entered upon (p. 731).

A diagram is given to show the most convenient forms for tankards, with reference to facility of pouring, on lines similar to those on which Christopher Dresser constructed his teapots, a decade or two later (p. 733).

Altogether, Redgrave found ample scope for criticism. He talks of decorative *"shams"*, and "the age of putty, papier maché, and gutta percha", wherein "the florid and the gaudy take the place of the simple and the true" (p. 713). In furniture,

bunches of fruit, flowers, game, and utensils of various kinds in swags and festoons of the most massive size and the boldest impost [are found all over] attached indiscriminately and without meaning to bedsteads, sideboards, bookcases, pier-glasses, etc., rarely carved from the members of the work itself, but merely applied as so much putty-work or papier-maché might be. The laws of ornament are as completely set at defiance as those of use and convenience (p. 721).

Grates are marred by a "tendency to do too much" by way of ornament; some French carpets "might as well be florid designs for the decoration of ceilings, if such a false system could be applied anywhere" (pp. 726–27). As a general conclusion,

there can be no doubt that half the ornament in the Great Exhibition, and consequently the labour expended on it, is in excess; that is to say, that a better effect might have been produced without it; and this wasted labour might have been bestowed on the more careful completion of simpler designs, to the enriching of the manufacturer, and the great advantage of the public taste (p. 727).

This criticism was endorsed by others of the group. Owen Jones said that

we have no principles, no unity; the architect, the upholsterer, the paper-stainer, the weaver, the calico-printer, and the potter, run each their independent course; each struggles fruitlessly, each produces in art novelty without beauty, or beauty without intelligence.[37]

Digby Wyatt was struck, like many others, by the superior beauty shown in the products of other peoples less technically advanced: "It was but natural that we should be startled when we found that in consistency of design in industrial art, those we had been too apt to regard as almost savages were infinitely our superiors."[38]

A third member of the group, *Ralph Nicholson Wornum*, compiler of the 1846 official catalogue of the National Gallery, and lecturer on art in the School of Design in 1848, wrote that "there is nothing new in the Exhibition in ornamental design; not a scheme, not a detail that has not been treated over and over again in the ages that are gone"; he found "that the taste of the producers generally is uneducated, and that in nearly all cases where this is not so, the influence of France is paramount in the European productions."[39]

When giving the reason for the deplorable lowering of standards in design, Richard Redgrave, seemingly influenced by Ruskin, writes nostalgically in his report of the old craftsman whose hand and mind "wrought together . . . from feelings of piety, from love of his labours, or from the desire of fame," before industrial division of labour was known—"motives hardly known to the artists of this class in our days . . . . Wherever ornament is wholly effected by machinery, it is certainly the most degraded in style and execution" (p. 710). Redgrave's remedy does not, like that of Ruskin, break with the established system; he argues for a reform of the position of designer and craftsman within it. The division of labour between these two he obviously takes for granted, imagining a numerous class of art-workmen, whose

province is quite apart from the imaginative, and all that *he* requires [in the way of education] is a full acquaintance with the *technical means* of art, such as drawing, modelling, chasing, painting, etc. In these he cannot be too fully educated (p. 748).

The members of this group should be the executives, raised above the standard of mere "hands" by their superior knowledge of their craft. The master mind, however, would be the top-hatted designer, an artist who has thoroughly mastered the technical language of art, and the general principles of art and its application. The special technical knowledge needed by him "is speedily acquired in any branch of manufacture to which he may devote his attention". For both classes, however, it would be desirable that schools should be organised not only [as] schools of design, but in some degree workshops, where the specialties of design may be fully explained, and the due application of ornamental art to manufacture thoroughly exemplified and carried into practice

for the mutual benefit of designer and art-workman alike (p. 748). But a new scheme would have to begin from scratch, and so "society also must be prepared to contribute more largely than heretofore to public education in ornamental art, and taste must be disseminated by every available means" (p. 711).

Reform was in the air, and Wyatt was certainly right when he said that the Exhibition must be regarded as an "extraordinary stimulant" that alone could awaken "all our energies" so that "men's minds are now earnestly directed to the subject of restoring to symmetry all that had fallen into disorder."[40]

Part III: The Eighteen-Fifties

DEPARTMENTAL ACTIVITIES AND A NEW LITERATURE OF DESIGN

The entire World Exhibition of 1851 was the expression of a desire on the part of its organisers to measure the material progress of this generation. In the words of the Prince Consort,

> the Exhibition of 1851 is to give us a true test and a living picture of the point of development at which the whole of mankind has arrived ...., and a new starting-point from which all nations will be able to direct their further exertions.[41]

The quotation has been taken from his speech at a banquet in promotion of the Exhibition, a speech which quite clearly brings out the high ideals directing the actions of the Prince and his circle. However, the great event also achieved a tremendous commercial importance. Here the products of all countries were seen together for comparison for the first time, and here the strong position of British industry in many fields must have seemed truly impressive.

Not, however, artistically impressive; the complaints of Richard Redgrave and of Digby Wyatt were echoed by others, and the opinion is universally expressed by various critics in contemporary journals that French taste dominated in those fields of manufacture where taste counted for anything, especially in furniture and textiles. There arose a strong desire to redress this defect, to raise British products once more to the level of their former excellence, and to recapture for them a market abroad which had been lost since the hey-day of Anglomania on the Continent in the latter half of the 18th century. Forces within the Government and the Administration felt this to be a public concern, and efforts were made to extend and reorganise the existing Schools of Design on a grand scale.

The leader of the new governmental attempt at reform which actually followed the Great Exhibition, was to be Henry Cole, who became prime mover in the establishment of a new Department of Practical Art, which was now organised under the Board of Trade. It was to include the old Schools of Design, where teaching should now be based on principles similar to those developed by the pioneers in the 'forties, and applied by Redgrave in his *Supplementary Report*. The Department must be considered as an entirely new project, which fostered important activities even outside the field of the old Schools of Design, especially with regard to general education and the building up of a central art collection, which later grew into the Victoria and Albert Museum.

Cole's connection with the administration of the new Department dates back to the autumn of 1851, when he was offered the secretaryship of the Schools of Design by Lord Granville. When one considers his previous activities in related fields, this was a natural choice. Apart from his art-books and the part played by him in Summerly's Art-Manufactures, *The Journal of Design*, the Society of Arts, and the Great Exhibition itself, his reports and letters to the Parliamentary Committee of 1849 contained a series of useful suggestions for reform of the organisation and the system of teaching in the Schools of Design. He particularly stressed the importance of a simplified administration so as to leave responsibility in fewer hands, and offered some very straightforward criticism together with suggestions for a reform directed towards more practical teaching.

Cole's final appointment came through in January, 1852, when at his own request the name of the school was changed to the Department of Practical Art. The huge committee formerly in charge was abolished, and the Department organised under the Board of Trade, with Cole at the head under the title of Superintendent; Richard Redgrave was made to work beside him as Art-Superintendent, an arrangement which Cole seems slightly to have regretted. Then, to follow Cole's account,

the new department's work was divided into two broad divisions, the one affecting elementary instruction in drawing and modelling, the other affecting advanced instruction, and its special bearing upon ornamental art.[42]

In 1852, the entire department was moved from Somerset House to Marlborough House, where Cole arranged a "Chamber of Horrors" to contain objects which illustrated departures from the principles taught in the departmental classes. In *Household Words* Dickens gave a very Dickensian suggestion of the popular reaction to this new arrangement,[43] and Christopher Dresser, the designer, later gave some detailed information about it:

we had scissors formed as birds, which separated into halves every time that the scissors were opened; candle-sticks formed as human beings, with the candle fitting into the top of a chimney-pot hat or into the head; egg-cups formed as birds' nests; plaid fabrics bearing check patterns so large that it almost required two persons to wear the same pattern in order that the whole design be seen; carpets on which ponds of water were drawn with water-lilies floating upon them; and other absurdities equally offensive to good taste.[44]

He might just as well have said "offensive to good reason", since the fury of Cole and his associates was raised to equal heat by logical incongruities and by fallings-off in aesthetic qualities. It was this lack of toleration for the fanciful whim which irritated Dickens into ridiculing Cole with his unflinching and—as Dickens thought—unimaginative adherence to rule. Having poured his venom on the young Pre-Raphaelitic movement, the great writer was no more inclined to let any new "arty" ideas take hold of the lesser arts, and so change the world around him: he wrote of Cole "that he overdoes it" and hoped that they would be able to "meet at last at some halfway house where there are flowers on the carpets, and a little standing-room for Queen Mab's Chariot among the Steam Engines",[45] and there can be little doubt that "the third gentleman" in Chapter II of his *Hard Times*, is modelled, somewhat viciously maybe, upon our clever Superintendent:

The third gentleman now stepped forth. A mighty man at cutting and drying, he was; a government officer; .... And he had it in charge from high authority to bring about the great public-office Millennium, when Commissioners should reign upon earth.

This gentleman then proceeds to put questions to the class of youngsters into which he has entered, as follows:

"Suppose you were going to carpet a room. Would you use a carpet having a representation of flowers upon it?"

There being a general conviction by this time that "No, sir!" was always the right answer to this gentleman, the chorus of No was very strong. Only a few feeble stragglers said Yes; among them Sissy Jupe.

"Girl number twenty," said the gentleman, smiling in the calm strength of knowledge.

Sissy blushed and stood up.

"So you would carpet your room—or your husband's room, if you were a grown woman, and had a husband—with representations of flowers, would you?" said the gentleman. "Why would you?"

"If you please, sir, I am very fond of flowers," returned the girl.

"And is that why you would put tables and chairs upon them, and have people walking over them with heavy boots?"

"It wouldn't hurt them, sir. They wouldn't crush and wither if you please, sir. They would be the pictures of what was very pretty and pleasant, and I would fancy—"

"Ay, ay, ay! But you mustn't fancy," cried the gentleman, quite elated by coming so happily to his point. "That's it! You are never to fancy."

"You are not, Cecilia Jupe," Thomas Gradgrind solemnly repeated, "to do anything of that kind."

"Fact, fact, fact!" said the gentleman. And "Fact, fact, fact!" repeated Thomas Gradgrind.

"You are to be in all things regulated and governed," said the gentleman, "by fact."[46]

However, in spite of the novelist's scorn, the new Department, which had been created as the expression of official will, soon consolidated its position on all sides. Through a series of purchases a collection of art was formed, to become the nucleus of the later Victoria and Albert Museum; £5,000 had also been granted to purchase works from the Great Exhibition, and a committee was charged with this duty, appointed by the President of the Board of Trade. The members of the committee were J. R. Herbert, R. A. (of the Schools of Design), Redgrave, Pugin, Owen Jones, and Cole. In 1853 the scope of the Department's activities became considerably enlarged, and its name was changed to "The Department of Science and Art". In 1857 this body was finally moved to South Kensington, where rooms were provided for the exhibition of the extensive collections now under the Department's charge, and also for its collections of books. In the same year the Department was transferred from the Board of Trade to the Council of Education.[47]

Briefly, this was the early history of the new official establishment for the improvement of industrial design in England. It is important not to confuse its aims with those of the later Arts and Crafts movement; it should be remembered that the Department took for granted the existing conditions of industrial machine production, and that its teaching was in the main directed towards supplying industry with capable designers.

Now this was a policy which met with serious objection in the new ideas of John Ruskin, which were gaining support at this very time. As will be seen later, Ruskin objected on principle to the whole system of mechanised production of artistic goods, and his position was gradually becoming so influential that it will be of interest to reproduce a few statements to show how unanimous responsible men in the Department were in their acceptance of existing conditions—and consequently in their opposition to Ruskin's views.

Certainly, a cultivator of the Fine Arts like Richard Redgrave, R. A., could allow himself to show a certain amount of Ruskinian regret, and bewail "the mechanical production of ornament" as "another evil condition of ornamental art in the present day"; he spoke of "the dull uniformity of the machine" and the "mechanical repetition of art", tending "in its consequences, to enslave the ornamentist"; but he also felt that the "perfect cure" of this evil was "no doubt, hopeless ... because it is caused by the wants and means of society in its present state, and has its origin in the very nature of our manufacturing processes as ministering to those wants."[48]

Opposed to Redgrave's reluctant acquiescence, there is Wornum's remark that the illumination of manuscripts must have been "an inordinate waste of labour over trifles",[49] and his conviction that "if we can but establish the essential quality of all decoration, taste, the rising generation will have nothing to fear from the rivalry or the prestige of past ages." He was writing of "Specimens of Jordan's machine-carving", and says of them that if "the most delicate touches only" were given by the hand, they would be "quite equal to the general average of that executed wholly by hand .... the saving of labour and expense must be enormous."[50]

A standard of "general average" was, maybe, not a sufficiently worthy aim, and Gottfried Semper showed a keener feeling for the problem than is demonstrated by Wornum in his somewhat superficial acceptance of modernity. The German architect was worried:

What will be the consequences of the depreciation of matter owing to its treatment by machines, to surrogates and to all these new inventions? What will be the consequences of the depreciation through the same causes, of work, of pictorial, sculptural or other endowments? I obviously do not mean their depreciation in price, but in importance, in ideal meaning. Have not the new Houses of Parliament in London been made unsightly by the machines? How can time or science bring law and order into this hitherto complete confusion, how prevent the general depreciation from extending to the object which has really been produced by hand in the old way, so that nothing is found in it but affectation, antiquarianism, eccentricity and caprice?[51]

(This was, of course, what later happened to William Morris.) Semper could give no decisive solution to his problem—to him, as to Jones, the age "is like a Chinese eating with a knife and fork;" but he had faith in progress:

I do not by any means deplore the general state of things, of which these are only the less important symptoms; on the contrary, I am sure that they will sooner or later develop happily in all directions to the prosperity and honour of society.[52]

A veteran from the old Schools of Design, George Wallis, certainly took no higher view of existing conditions than Ruskin did, but he emphatically protested against

the proposition so frequently maintained, that machinery has been the immediate cause of the effort after low priced shams and imitations, and that therefore machinery is to be repudiated in the production of artistic results... What is our machinery? Is it not another mode of applying the ingenuity and inventive power with which man has been endowed...? Shall we repudiate the use of the steam-engine, and still employ the water-wheel as a motive power?

In opposition to one of Ruskin's pet arguments, Wallis flatly denied

that the use of machinery deadens the energies of the worker, renders him too a machine, and lessens his interest in his work. Experience proves the contrary, and it is most unhesitatingly declared.... that the workers [at machines] are, without exception, the most intelligent of their class.

In fact, the more complicated the machine, the more intelligent its operative. So,

our chief reliance is on our mechanical skill and our science, which, as a duality, are nearly perfect, but as a *trine* or complete figure, are wanting in one great essential,—the external quality of beauty as an outward manifestation based on aesthetic principles—in short, Art in its fullest and most complete sense.[53]

To complete this "trine" had now fallen to the lot of the new Department of Practical Art.

This Department, then, settled in 1852 at Marlborough House under the joint directorship of Cole and Redgrave, was organised on lines expressed in the official addresses of the two Superintendents, delivered at Marlborough House in November.[54]

As has been already noted, the field of activities had now been substantially enlarged, compared with the old Schools of Design; one of the important new enterprises was the instruction of the general public in the theory and practice of design, mainly through drawing-schools; this step was taken, Cole explains, because of a new conviction that "the improvement of manufactures is .... altogether dependent upon the public sense of the necessity of it, and the public ability to judge between what is good and bad in art"— much the same argument that is urged for similar purposes by the Council of Industrial Design today. Cole's contemporaries took a very generous view of the matter, "the Government" having "broadly affirmed the principle that elementary knowledge of form and colour shall become part of the national education."

Teaching in the new schools included special classes in "Artistic Anatomy, Practical Construction, Wood engraving for ladies only, Porcelain Painting, decoration of Woven Fabrics and flat surfaces generally, and the ornamental treatment of Metals". There was also a class for *"Architectural Details* and *Practical Construction"*, where among other things "Practical Geometry and Geometric Construction" was taught as "applied to Carpentry, Joiners' Work, Masons' Work, Plastering and the various branches of Constructive Architecture; Upholstery, and Interior Decoration." Redgrave explained, in his address, that in such and other classes

the student will be able to obtain information; first, as to all the principles of fitness and choice which should govern the application of Ornament to the special fabric or manufacture; and, secondly, as to all those peculiar processes of Manufacture, whether by the hand or the machine, which are to control and regulate his labours, together with all improvements, chemical, mechanical, or manipulative, which from time to time arise to change the laws of production.

The practical instructions would be completed by "lectures, on the history and styles of Ornament—on Chemistry, Botany, Metallurgy, etc, connected with Art" and by museum and library studies.

Redgrave's address, and the one he gave the year after at the opening session of the Department of Science and Art,[55] do not offer anything startling by way of theory; they are valuable mainly because they give the new, recognized principles in brief and firm statements, showing how they set the standard for official teaching at last. Redgrave stresses the necessity for guiding principles, and advocates study and adaptation of natural form to use, material, and technique of production; and we have seen how a deeper understanding of the various factors that go to create good design was to be fostered in the school through a teaching balanced evenly between theory and practical instruction, with insight into the technical sciences as a necessary complement, to enable the designer to keep abreast of progress within the various industries by turning each new invention to artistic account.

The practical teaching, carried on in classes set up *inter alia* in metal-work and embroidery, was not to be a permanent feature. Cole's autobiography is not clear on this point, and other sources are difficult to come by; but it seems not unlikely that governmental instruction was felt to interfere with the various forms of apprenticeship which still existed in various industries, since at least as late as 1842–43 apprenticeship was the rule "in by far the majority of the [miscellaneous] Trades and Manufactures".[56] At any rate, Cole was already making atonement, as it almost seems, in an address of 16th November, 1857, saying that

some years' experience and earnest efforts have now shown conclusively that State interference in any special technical teaching, founded upon the assumption of trade requirements, does not succeed. I confess myself to have been at one time of a contrary opinion, and to have thought that it was both possible and expedient that effect should be given to the professions originally made in establishing the School of Design.[57]

In his *Academies of Art* Nikolaus Pevsner seems to suggest that the scheme for practical teaching at the Department was somehow connected with Gottfried Semper's attendance there. He writes

the new classes for 'metals, jewellery, and enamels, ... fabrics, embroidery, lace and paperstaining' [that is the whole establishment for practical teaching] were discontinued as early as 1856. Semper left for Zürich in 1855, and after a short time the establishment was hardly more than a training ground for future teachers of art.[58]

It is certainly true that practical instruction *was* given up; moreover, it is also true that at this time the Department ceased to be a centre from which new and stimulating ideas would emanate; any growth of ideas which we may find in the latter half of the century originated with single artists or with more or less permanent groups of artists, like the various guilds and societies. However, it seems unwarranted to suggest a connection between this change and Semper's departure: the principle of practical instruction had been topical within the Schools of Design almost from the start— we need only recall Dyce's efforts in that field; and as to the growth of a comprehensive theory of design in relation to art-manufacture, we have traced important contributions made in England all the way back through the 'forties. I do not know what previous experience might warrant the influence in England which Pevsner has seemed willing to ascribe to him. On the contrary, recalling his late date of arrival, it seems to me more reasonable to suggest that Semper was himself influenced by his new English acquaintances; and his small treatise on *Wissenschaft, Industrie und Kunst,* published in 1852, from which quotations have been given above, must consequently also be classed as one among many other very interesting treatises on this subject, which appeared in England during the years immediately following the Great Exhibition—and evidently one which was intended to make new lines of thought, developed in England, known to a German public: the book was written in German, and its subtitle describes it as *"Vorschläge zur Anregung nationalen Kunstgefühles bei dem Schluss der Londoner Industrie-Ausstellung".*[59]

With this book of Semper's we pass on to a number of similar writings published in the years following 1851, which contain material of interest for theoretical study. Many of them had a strong and widespread influence throughout the Victorian era and were valuable because they brought together more or less scattered ideas and made them accessible to a wider public; but on the score of originality they have little to offer that had not been said before. In spite of some extremely apposite and lucid statements, this is also true of the book by Semper just mentioned, where, without noteworthy additions, we find the now well-known principles of conventionalised pattern built on natural form, and so on. He expressed the general admiration for the beauty of Indian textiles, and stressed the importance of trying to improve the taste of the general public so as to make it demand a higher standard of design. Nor is it uncharacteristic of this period to read of his admiration for the functional lines of purely useful objects exhibited at the Crystal Palace—an observation which he made in common with others.

In a vein similar to that of Semper, Wyatt had given, in 1852, a lecture entitled *An Attempt to define the Principles which should determine Form in the decorative Arts;*[60] his impressive folios on *Industrial Arts of the Nineteenth Century* appeared in 1851, and the one on *Metal-Work* the next year. Wornum published a small volume called *Analysis of Ornament*, subtitled *An Introduction to the Study of the History of Ornament*, in 1856, while after Redgrave's death his son compiled from his various writings a *Manual of Design* in 1876. Other writings appeared as well, mostly of an archaeological nature, but not one of them equalled in magnificence and thoroughness the *Grammar of Ornament*, written by Owen Jones, and published in 1856; this was undoubtedly the work the influence of which was most strongly felt throughout the rest of the Victorian era. It contained one hundred coloured plates, and twenty essays on various styles, from the primitive ones of the Pacific to the traditional ones of the East and West up to modern times.[61]

This magnificent volume contained also, by way of introduction, a list of 37 "General Principles in the Arrangement of Form and Colour, in Architecture and the decorative Arts, which are advocated throughout this Work"[62]. These general principles, or "Propositions" as they were also called, are given in full in Appendix II; they may be taken to represent the ultimate codification of principles developed since the first Parliamentary Committee was established to look into the question of Industrial Design in England in 1836; thus they close a period of twenty years' research into laws governing the application of design to the products of contemporary industry.

Seen as a unity, Jones's propositions represent an intellectual construction built on research into phenomena in nature and art, and carried out in a scientific spirit of analysis. On major points, they include known themes: universal education in the Arts (proposition 37), study of the principles to be discovered in the art of the past without slavishly copying its forms (36), an insistence on conventional treatment of natural form (13); in the words of the introduction, "the future progress of Ornamental Art may be best secured by engrafting on the experience of the past the knowledge we may obtain by a return to Nature for fresh inspiration." The present must be wholly discarded—"If we would return to a more healthy condition, we must even be as little children or as savages; we must get rid of the acquired and artificial, and return to and develop natural instincts." This last was written in a chapter on *Ornament of Savage Tribes*, which incidentally forms an early example of appreciation of truly primitive art. The idea that a natural instinct for ornamental art really did exist, had been firmly established earlier by Dyce, and Wornum had called ornament "one of the mind's necessities", consequently to be exploited as "an essential element in commercial prosperity".[63]

Jones's conception of the true quality of ornamental art involved harmony, balance and repose (3), resulting in a feeling of completeness (4), obtained through subdivision of form (7), and a nice proportion of parts (9), in a geometrical construction (8). As authorities for these propositions, he later quoted Vitruvius, Eastlake, and Wyatt;[64] one might call this the academic, traditional part of Jones's theory. Propositions Nos. 6 and 10 are his own formal arbitrations, suggested through studies of natural form and oriental art. For 1 no authority is quoted, while the content of 2 is sanctioned by passages from Pugin, Ruskin, Wyatt, and Seroux d'Agincourt and was, like its predecessor, an idea widely accepted at the time. 11 and 12 are built on "Oriental Practice" and "Natural Law". Those from 14 to 34 deal with colour. Of them, 14, 16, 17, 28, and probably 15 as well, are derived from historic study, while 14 is also sanctioned by study of nature.[65] 21 is based on the study of Moorish art, 22, 29, 30, and 31 have Indian authority.[66] 18 is founded on the Chromatic Equivalents of George Field, who published them in his *Chromatography* in 1835. Field founded his theories on Newton's prismatic experiments, but reduced the seven primaries of that author to the three recognised today, namely red, yellow, and blue; he was then able to prove the other four to be combinations of the three primary ones. Jones's proposition No. 18 points directly back to him, and the rest of the unascribed ones, though the parallel is less immediately obvious, have probably a common origin in Field's work as well.

Such were the inspirations for the work which, in the phrase of Lewis F. Day, "marks a point, and a turning-point, in the history of English ornament". True enough, still according to Day, his principles "were many of them not principles at all", and the good they did was more in the nature of "tips" to "manufacturers, decorators, and designers, who were floundering in the depths of degradation in which he found the minor arts of design". But "no man did more than he towards clearing the ground for us, and so making possible the new departures which we have made since his time." Jones had greater influence than Ruskin and Pugin, because they were not listened to by manufacturers as he was.[67]

However, in spite of its many admirable qualities, the *Grammar* seems to me to suffer from a lack of spontaneity, of frank and genuine artistic feeling. This has somehow been lost among all the theories, where small room is left for fanciful "little children or savages" with their free and easy "natural instincts". In unguarded moments, when their usual seriousness was in abeyance, Owen Jones and his friends might sometimes have caught a glimpse of such possibilities, but they were still for some time to remain outside the reach of English design.

We have followed, through roughly two decades, the development of theories of design, as well as of institutions to teach them. It has been possible to trace the origin and development of some permanent motives, such as the principle of inspiration from natural form, manifested in design through a process of conventionalisation, and the study of ancient art for the extraction of principles to direct such a process.

It has become clear how these principles owed their victory in official instruction to the activities of a relatively small group of men, who assumed an attitude of co-operation with the forces of a mechanised industry. Their outlook on social structure, class division, and so forth, was not affected by those radical ideas which were at the same time developed by Ruskin, and which later were to colour many designers' attitude to their art; our pioneers were conservatives at least in so far as their whole scheme for a reform of design was planned to work within the already existing social framework, with its established habits of producing and consuming. Division of labour was to them a tacitly accepted fact, and was reflected in their own principles by a division between manufacturer, designer, and art-workman. They were themselves bourgeois; at the time when Ruskin pleaded for the soul of the working man, their social struggle, as far as it went, was for the recognition of the designer as a respected member of the middle class, to take his seat on Parnassus beside his top-hatted cousin from the Royal Academy.

They were also bourgeois in their view of design, which in its fundamentals was adapted to the needs of contemporary middle class life; there was but scant discussion of the habits and arrangements of daily life which are inevitably and eternally connected with it, and no wish to create a material standard which would tend to break up existing conventions—as Pugin had done with his mediae-valism, as Morris was going to do, and as le Corbusier and others have done in our own time. It is true that in view of those often surprisingly modern-sounding statements of which some have been quoted, one might expect the works of these men to bear some formal relation to the products of the *Bauhaus*, or the Continental functionalism of the 'thirties; but in expecting this, it would be necessary to forget the enormous importance which the Victorians assigned to the narrative and associative elements in all art, by which a piece of furniture could be made to tell a story, and which in con-temporary painting and sculpture extolled *sentiment* as a main object of interest.

It is thus perfectly obvious that, however much they might be capable of recognising the aesthetic value of pure colour and form, the early Victorian *avant-gardistes* regarded *ornament* as an essen-tial part of design—as did Owen Jones's fifth proposition which says that "construction *should* be decorated" (italics are mine). Once this principle is recognised, it is easily seen how profoundly our reformers were influenced by current Victorian tendencies, in spite of every statement of theirs which might, on the face of it, be quoted to the opposite effect. Their demand for "fitness" and for "appro-priateness" of design more often than not signifies that the decora-tion should correspond in meaning to the use for which the decor-ated object was designed. It is manifest, I think, that they loved ornament for its own sake, and showed a tendency to apply it everywhere, at the cost of purely formal and linear effects of beauty in the object itself.

In this particular connection it is difficult not to remark on what must inevitably seem a certain shallowness of thought. For instance, Owen Jones speaks of the possibilities for a new architecture to rise out of fresh ornamental forms, saying that "if we could only arrive at the invention of a new termination to a means of support, one of the most difficult points would be accomplished,"—

and holding (in full harmony with Ruskin, by the way) that "by the ornament of a building we can judge more truly of the creative power which the artist has brought to bear upon the work." A little further on he expresses his opinion that "it is the decoration of .... structural features which gives the characteristics of style."[68]

We find the same tendency in every single one of his co-operators. Wyatt talks of "attempt at novelty", which among other things "must be executed in subservience to .... the condition of emotions dependent on a legitimate and sensible association of idea, founded upon a study of all that has been done in the best ages of the past."[69] He also wrote that

the true office of simplicity is to limit form and ornament to a correct expression of whatever may be the predominant sentiment intended to be conveyed by any object, and to reject all that is extraneous to that sentiment.[70]

He also, like Jones and Ruskin, ascribed a high degree of importance to sculpture in architecture. Even Gottfried Semper does not differ in the least, when, in the art of the East he regrets the lack of "individual expression, the language, the higher phonetic beauty, the soul", which would be obtainable

as soon as the object ceases to be only an end in itself and has some use or purpose. Tritons, Nereids, and Nymphs will always be meaningful by a well, Venus and the Graces by a mirror, trophies and combats with arms.[71]

No shadow of doubt should be allowed to remain on this point; and so, even at the risk of being tiresome, I must finally direct the reader's attention to Redgrave's comments on the sideboard illustrated in *Fig. 13*. The criticism—a long one—is taken from his *Report on Design* and reads as follows:

The sideboard, carved in walnut, as here shown, and which is exhibited in the French Court by Fourdinois ...., is an apt illustration of ornament having a just and characteristic significance. This piece of furniture is of rare excellence and merit in design, and of skilful and artistic execution as to carving, and, although of a highly decorative character, is fitted for the purpose for which it is intended. Six dogs, emblematical of the chace, resting

on a floor of inlaid wood, support the slab, which has a simple carved moulding along its front, and is inlaid in geometric forms. The dogs are not merely
imitative, but are treated as a part of an ornamented bracket or console, thus
composed architecturally for bearing and support. Above the slab, standing
on four pedestals, are female figures, gracefully designed as emblems of the
four quarters of the world, each bearing the most useful production of their
climate as contributions to the feast. Thus Europe has wine; Asia, tea; Africa,
coffee; and America, the sugar-cane.

Also, we find "products of the chace", and "a framed picture of
rare fruits, giving an opportunity to enliven the work by the addition of colour, without militating against good taste". Then there
are the urchins on the top "with the implements of the vineyard and
of agriculture", and on—or probably better, in—the pediment, which
is "broken in the manner of the Renaissance", there is "a figure of
Plenty crowning the group." Then,

The upright line of the back is gracefully varied at the sides, and constructively strengthened by carved brackets, above which are terminal
figures bearing the implements of fishery on the one side and of the
chace on the other.

In addition to all this,

two brackets on the side compartments between the figures give an opportunity for placing silver plate in a position for display. The ornamental parts of
this piece of furniture are carved throughout in a masterly manner, and in a bold
and free style; it is consistent as a whole, and free from puerilities, and, while it is
thoroughly fitted for its purpose as a sideboard, it is at the same time of a highly
ornamental character, without any of its decoration being overdone or thrown
away. It corresponds in its constructive form with the Renaissance of the 15th
century—in the style of its carvings rather with the works of the 13th; the
gates of Ghiberti having evidently supplied the idea of the groups of fruit
and implements which fill the panels; and it may be remarked as a fault, that
it has been overlooked that the relief in Ghiberti's work was suited to metal,
the ornament standing beyond the face of the framing of the panel; but in
adapting it to wood this should have been modified so as to bring the impost
of the carving within the surface; such faults, however, are trifling in a
work otherwise of great ability. The care which has been taken to keep
all the ornamental details in the same scale throughout is an additional merit,
and the wood has been judiciously chosen as to colour and grain.[72]

I trust this lengthy quotation may be excused for the insight it yields, and for the valuable way in which it clarifies some of the theories previously discussed. It will be understood that the decoration of this piece is as a whole an admirable example of that appropriateness of design which refers, as we shall now fully understand, first and foremost to the story-telling part of an object. The six emblematic dogs are examples of natural form adapted to ornamental purposes, since they are "composed architecturally for bearing and support". The necessity for abstract beauty of line is taken care of by the graceful "upright line of the back", and there is plenty of inspiration from nature to be found in the flowers, the fruit and the "products of the chace" so profusely applied to all the spare surfaces of the furniture. There is economy and balance of ornament, with none of it "thrown away", and, whereas it is not for us to discuss the correctness of Redgrave's stylistic analysis of the piece, it is evidently in itself an example of study and exploitation—not copying—of the ancient styles. Finally, the principle that ornament should be fitted to the material in which it is executed, is illustrated in a negative manner by the Ghiberti-inspired panels.

In the architectural field, Owen Jones realised that his own generation had

little hope that we are destined to see more than the commencement of a change; the architectural profession is at the present time too much under the influence of past education on the one hand, and too much influenced by an ill-informed public on the other.[73]

The truth of his words is illustrated to excess by works of contemporary architects and designers who tried to break away. I draw attention only to a single example among Owen Jones's own work, illustrated in Wyatt's article on Ironwork in the *Journal of Design (Fig. 14)*. The illustration represents a cast-iron shop-front, which was put into the older house of Chappell's, the music-sellers in New Bond Street. Wyatt holds the balcony to be the least successful part, its rather clumsy form illustrating "the great difficulty always met with in uniting materials which require such various proportions as stone or brick and iron". All the same, he calls

the effect of the whole.... most satisfactory, and we feel convinced that such combinations of talent, were they more common in the "highways and byways" of London, would materially elevate the style of our now anything but admirable street architecture.[74]

Now this shop-front exhibits the traditional division between column, arch, and architrave; afraid or unwilling to do away with capital and base, Jones has striven to give them new appearance through the application of conventionalised floral forms, where a modernist would have realised the superfluity of the very members themselves, and left them out altogether as unessential for structural purposes. The arch, even, with its carefully ornamented spandrils, is probably equally superfluous from a structural point of view, the iron architrave being seemingly of sufficient strength for all reasonable purposes. In the balcony we note the effort to create something fresh in the ornamental "frieze", reminiscent of Gothic machicolations, while the iron rail exhibits that peculiar dryness which so easily killed all life in even the most well-intentioned geometric design of the *avant-gardistes;* the capital marked A is another example of an effort to give a new life to an old tradition, while the corner post of the balcony itself has fallen back on what seems to be pure stylistic imitation—an akroterion in a slightly surprising framing, and adapted to the wrong purpose.

It seems to me that these two examples give the final understanding of the true position and limitation, as well as the achievement, of the pioneer group. With minds embedded in a decaying tradition, they were led on, by a yearning for some new device by which to rescue contemporary design from its obvious state of confusion, to visualise nothing more startling than the infusion of new ornamental life into the existing framework of a stale convention.

THE ETHICS OF ORNAMENT

John Ruskin

Books have been written on almost every aspect of Ruskin's thought, and in Victorian aesthetics his position is so dominating that hardly any treatise on English art of that period can entirely pass him by. True, he never took up at any length the theoretical study of design; but his general attitude to art implies in itself an opposition to the manner in which the new establishments at Somerset House were directed. Here and there in his vast *oeuvre* I have also been able to discover short passages, verbal side-glances, and remarks that go far to build up a specific Ruskinian theory of design; its emphasis is fundamentally so different from that of the contemporary Henry Cole group that a few pages must be sacrificed to explain it.

We have seen how in various enterprises, mostly of an official character, a reform of design was sought for within the existing contemporary bourgeois convention; the basic ideas in Ruskin's philosophy went far beyond, even to the point of questioning the value of that convention itself.

It may be that the starting-point for any consideration of Ruskinian philosophy is to be found in his own passionate love of natural beauty, so strong that in reality it amounted to nothing less than a cult. His travels as a child and later as a young man had brought him into contact with the most splendid scenery of Europe, and at home he spent hours every day watching the sunset or changes in the weather; the overwhelming influence which this interest achieved in forming his outlook on life was substantiated by a close study of botany, geology, zoology, and even meteorology. The beauty of unspoilt nature, or natural beauty enhanced by the traditional activities of man—tilling of the fields, building of beautiful churches and peaceful hamlets, farmhouses and noble manors, or stately cities adorned with picturesque squares and ornate houses where the richness and beauty of natural form would be represented in solid, unspoilt material and rich ornament—this harmonious combination of nature and art became to him the one and only setting for a dignified human existence, as well as a natural outcome of it. He had studied scenes like these in the Europe of his youth; in the villages of England, in the cathedral cities of France, and the towns of northern Italy he had still found things relatively unchanged by advancing industrialisation, or by restoring antiquarians. It was under the influence of places like these that he became attached to Gothic art and to the attitude of life which he felt was expressed in it. This again led to his rejection of the Classical tradition on moral grounds; his book *Stones of Venice* of 1851 marks the outstanding turning-point in this respect, and his line of argument here is one which in the main offers surprising parallels to the ideas pervading the writings of Welby Pugin a decade and a half earlier.[1] Like Pugin Ruskin found that the advance of the Renaissance meant a profanation of the arts, which now became expressive of moral laxity, ungodliness, and vanity; together with the new styles which followed it, it was based retrospectively on a heathen past, and of this no good could ever arise.

Also like Pugin, he felt that a reform of the arts would be impossible without some substantial change in the society of which art forms an integral part. His firm Protestant prejudice prevented him from seeking a solution based on a Catholic point of view;

instead, in analysing the process of art-production, he strongly stressed the element of human happiness and satisfaction to be expressed through it, and formed a completely original theory for a renaissance of the arts—considering first of all the conditions of the working man. Pugin had chosen Catholicism as his personal answer; to Ruskin, complete social reform became the universal and only possible remedy. But to both men the basic Christian virtues of love, charity, reverence, and adoration were fundamentals on which a new order would have to be built. All these they both found to be eminently expressed in Gothic art—hence their common valuation of this style as the basis for a new and general development of art in future times.

To Ruskin, then, Gothic art seemed to express priceless virtues—and this it did because it was built on the wholesome observation of forms and principles in nature; I should not hesitate to suggest that Ruskin's interest in Gothic was a rationalisation of his love of natural beauty. "The great Gothic spirit," he once explained, "is also noble in its hold of nature;" and this because

in that careful distinction of species, and richness of delicate and undisturbed organization, which characterize the Gothic design, there is the history of rural and thoughtful life, influenced by habitual tenderness, and devoted to subtle inquiry.[2]

Ruskin never became the advocate of a Neo-Gothic style copied from original mediaeval forms; it was the basic attitude of Gothic he wanted to recapture, and as the most essential part of it, he wanted to regain its noble "hold of nature". As in the case of Wordsworth, by whose works he must have been inspired on this point,[3] his deeply religious nature invested this relation with profound meaning; he felt that the "common and general sources of pleasure" which lie embodied in the charms of nature consisted "in a certain seal, or impress of divine work and character, upon whatever God has wrought in all the world".[4] It became consequently a matter of the utmost significance that beauty of this kind—or representations of it—should form an integral part of human life; for to him these "ideas of beauty" were "among the noblest which can be presented to the human mind, invariably exalting and purifying it according to their degree".[5]

There are two conclusions to be drawn from this statement: first, that man must shape his material surroundings in such a way that natural beauty is constantly kept before him—either in the form of rivers, and mountains, and living flowers and trees, or in beautiful artistic representation of such forms. The other deduction to be made points to the moral impact of all art, which in Ruskin's opinion becomes dependent upon its adherence to natural form: the contention "that art, so far as it was devoted to the record or the interpretation of nature, would be helpful and ennobling also"[6]—while he also "would fain be allowed to assume .... that forms which are *not* taken from natural objects *must* be ugly"[7]—and consequently morally objectionable in every way. On this point, at least, his reasonings led him to conform to a main principle of the Department of Science and Art, even if their respective points of departure were widely different. We shall later see how disagreement arose between them on the detailed application of this general idea.

Ruskin's well-known scepticism with regard to the problem of a novel form of architecture, must also be seen in relation to his insistence that this art should be rich in reference to natural form. As to the introduction of iron to any noticeable extent, he regretted it, feeling that "every idea respecting size, proportion, decoration, or construction, on which we are at present in the habit of acting or judging," depended on the presupposition of the traditional materials of "clay, wood, or stone". Since Ruskin felt "unable to escape the influence of these prejudices" and believed "that my readers will be equally so, it may be perhaps permitted to me to assume that true architecture does not admit iron as a constructive material." This was written in *The Seven Lamps of Architecture*, published in 1849; and at this time, despite his lack of enthusiasm for it, he yet anticipated some fundamental change; "the time is probably near when a new system of architectural laws will be developed, adapted entirely to metallic construction."[8]

However, on this point his feeling of resentment was soon to be changed into violent opposition; and the reason for this must be that in the Crystal Palace of the 1851 Exhibition he saw an eminent example of modern iron and glass construction; what he saw was not to his liking, and he deeply regretted the popular acclaim with which this effort of Joseph Paxton's was being welcomed.

Ruskin felt that the Palace in Hyde Park fell short on two points—first, because translucid glass and thin constructive iron frames were not materials sufficiently substantial to express architectural form; and "all noble architecture depends for its majesty on its form". But his second argument in criticizing the revolutionary structure, was far more important to him; he felt that it was sorely inexpressive of human imagination, and that "the quantity of thought it expresses" was "a single and very admirable thought of Sir Joseph Paxton's . . . . that it might be possible to build a greenhouse larger than ever greenhouse was built before. This thought, and some very ordinary algebra, are as much as all that glass can represent of human intellect".[9] He missed his architectural sculpture, his carved foliage, his saints and his beasts and birds lovingly wrought; the true architect, besides being a good builder, "must, somehow, tell us a fairy tale out of his head beside all this, else we cannot praise him for his imagination". The new architecture of iron and glass gave no scope for this. Ruskin could not—quite naturally at that time—envisage any other form of innovation; the one which he had seen, he could not endure; and so he advised the contemporary architect to cultivate his imagination in his art, to link it to the constructive forces, to the forms and materials of unspoilt nature. He also stressed very emphatically the value of traditional feeling, believing, as he told the architects, that if you

can get the noise out of your ears of the perpetual, empty, idle, incomparably idiotic talk about the necessity of some novelty in architecture, you will soon see that the very essence of a Style, properly so called, is that it should be practised *for ages*, and applied to all purposes; and that so long as any given style is in practice, all that is left for individual imagination to accomplish must be within the scope of that style, not in the invention of a new one.[10]

This shows how Ruskin advised architecture to reject the new technical advance of iron and glass in building, because it gave no scope for his first and fundamental demand for the exercise of human imagination in contact with the forms and primary materials of nature.

A second principle of fundamental importance for Ruskin's entire view of art has already been hinted at; I am referring to his ideas of ennobling and debasing labour which were expressed with brilliant force in the chapter on "The Nature of Gothic" in the second volume of *Stones of Venice*. His ideas on this subject were the immediate outcome of studies in Gothic ornament and architecture, but in the last resort even they were connected most intimately with his belief in the divinely inspired beauty of Nature.

Ruskin explained his love of the Gothic style by saying that it was "noble in its hold of nature"; we understand by now the deep significance of that phrase. A second point most strongly in its favour was that he held it to be an expression of thought and happiness in the working man. Speaking of the "servile ornament" of the Greek, Ninevite and Egyptian schools, he rejected them because in one way or another they indicated the subjection of the workman's mind, either to the rigid formal discipline of a stylistic convention, or the superior and equally rigid directions of a master builder. However,

in the mediaeval, or especially Christian, system of ornament, this slavery is done away with altogether; Christianity having recognized, in small things as well as in great, the individual value of every soul.[11]

Mediaeval ornament, he felt, both of the Romanesque and the Gothic school, was the outcome of individual effort by each sculptor. In the highly refined features of 13th century Gothic—in the slender, yet firm construction, enriched with the most delicate animal and floral ornament closely approaching natural form, in the solemn rows of statuary embodying the mysteries and legend of Christianity—in all this Ruskin saw insight, and love, and thoughtful action, and that proximity to God-inspired nature which he felt to be the one element without which art in the true sense could not exist.

In Gothic design all these properties were to be found; and they were expressed there not as a result of careful working to schedule, but because trust had been placed in the spiritual as well as manual capacity of each working man. With love of nature and religion in their hearts, and nature constantly before their eyes, these men worked with joy, and their very labour became to them a force for increasing their manual skill as well as their spiritual insight, these again in their turn leading to yet more noble and exalted forms of art.

Yet this could only be achieved, he acknowledged, at the risk of accepting the imperfect with the perfect, the bad work with the good; and in the very will to do this, lay the superiority of Gothic art to any other, since it offered an opportunity to all for developing their capacities:

it is, perhaps, the principal admirableness of the Gothic schools of architecture, that they thus receive the results of the labour of inferior minds; and out of fragments full of imperfection, and betraying that imperfection in every touch, indulgently raise up a stately and unaccusable whole.

The trust which Ruskin placed in the working man may be justified or not—but it forms the most beautiful element of his entire philosophy. "In the make and nature of every man," he goes on,

however rude or simple, whom we employ in manual labour, there are some powers for better things; some tardy imagination, torpid capacity of emotion, tottering steps of thought, there are, even at the worst. .... But they cannot be strengthened, unless we are content to take them in their feebleness .... if you will make a man of the working creature, you cannot make a tool. Let him but begin to imagine, to think, to try to do anything worth doing; and the engine-turned precision is lost at once. Out come all his roughness, all his dulness, all his incapability; shame upon shame, failure upon failure, pause after pause: but out comes the whole majesty of him also; and we know the height of it only when we see the clouds settling upon him. And, whether the clouds be bright or dark, there will be transfiguration behind and within them.

Ruskin's entire criticism of modern mechanical methods of production is embodied in this glorious piece of rhetoric. More than any previous system this seemed to him to enslave the worker's mind and kill his imagination; "the modern English mind", he said, was wrong in this, that it too intensely "desires, in all things, the utmost completion or perfection compatible with their nature." It insisted too much on "engine-turned precision", forcing men to work "with the accuracy of tools, to be precise and perfect in all their actions." For this, however, men were not intended, and by demanding too much in this direction, it must inevitably happen that "the whole human being be lost at last—a heap of sawdust, so far as its intellectual work in this world is concerned."

Any art, any design which has been produced at this cost, must be intrinsically bad, be it never so studied, never so costly; and so John Ruskin addresses himself to his fellow countryman, asking him once more to

look round this English room of yours, about which you have been proud so often, because the work of it was so good and strong, and the ornaments of it so finished. Examine again all those accurate mouldings, and perfect polishings, and unerring adjustments of the seasoned wood and tempered steel ... you have exulted over them, and thought how great England was, because her slightest work was done so thoroughly. Alas! If read rightly, these perfect-nesses are signs of a slavery in our England a thousand times more bitter and more degrading than that of the scourged African, or helot Greek.

Indeed, his previously mentioned antipathy to the contemporary architecture of glass and cast iron was also in part based on this, that he felt mining of iron and coal to be the most toilsome, unimaginative and debasing forms of work in existence. For this reason he wanted to restrict the use of iron to its lowest possible limit.

With his opinion of the supreme importance of ornamental art, Ruskin had scant sympathy with the activities conducted by the

Department of Practical Art. Admittedly, he shared with its pioneers an interest in ornament as such, and like them he saw in nature the main source of inspiration for the ornamentist. But the Governmental establishment was a part of trade politics, and Ruskin utterly despised anything like a commercial exploitation of the arts. His criticism was scathing, as when in later years he wrote that

the suddenly luminous idea that Art might possibly be a lucrative occupation, secured the submission of England to such instruction as, with that object, she could procure: and the Professorship of Sir Henry Cole at Kensington has corrupted the system of art-teaching all over England into a state of abortion and falsehood from which it will take twenty years to recover.[12]

It would lead us too far from the present context to go into a detailed account of Ruskin's ideas for a reform of human life. But it may in general be said that he first of all wanted to do away with all labour that was unhealthy according to his definition; firmly convinced that full command of what to produce rested with the consumer, he placed with him the responsibility for enforcing reform by regulating his habits of consumption; thus he must

1. Never encourage the manufacture of any article not absolutely necessary, in the production of which *Invention* has no share.
2. Never demand an exact finish for its own sake, but only for some practical or noble end.
3. Never encourage imitation or copying of any kind, except for the sake of preserving records of great works.[13]

These three rules would lead to a careful examination of wants, carried out in a spirit of benevolent consideration for one's fellow men; the result would be a greater simplicity of life, and the closing-down of a greater part of England's industrial workshops.

But it would also give added character to design. Freed from the sterile precision and impersonality of mechanised mass-production, it would regain the personal stamp which to Ruskin's mind was a characteristic of the best design in the past.

Living up to Ruskin's ideals, I said, would lead to a closing-down of the greater part of England's industrial workshops, and would set at nought the material and technical progress achieved through the Industrial Revolution. It should, however, be understood that Ruskin evidently visualised some sort of industry on a larger scale in his utopian conception of ideal England, and that he would allow machines to do necessary work of drudgery. But nothing must be done that would ruin the beauty of the countryside, and for

the establishment of manufactories needing the help of fire, [one should] .... find places elsewhere than in England, or at least in otherwise unserviceable parts of England.... to reduce such manufactures to their lowest limit, so that nothing may ever be made of iron that can as effectually be made of wood or stone; and nothing moved by steam that can be as effectually moved by natural forces—14

that is, by waterwheels and windmills and the like. As far as art was concerned, the problem was of course not to spoil the source from which it was to draw inspiration; and

all the lecturings, and teachings, and prizes, and principles of art, in the world [this must refer to the men at the Department in London], are of no use, so long as you don't surround your men with happy influences and beautiful things. It is impossible for them to have right ideas about colour, unless they see the lovely colours of nature unspoiled; impossible for them to supply beautiful incident and action in their ornament.15

As he also put it, "the beginning of art *is in getting our country clean, and our people beautiful.*"16

Besides being a threat to the beauty of the country, Ruskin also feared that mechanical production on any large scale would lead to separation of classes along undesirable lines, since the system inevitably involves that the few must plan work for the many:

we want one man to be always thinking, and another to be always working, and we call one a gentleman, and the other an operative; whereas the workman ought often to be thinking, and the thinker often to be working, and both should be gentlemen, in the best sense. As it is, we make both ungentle, the one envying, the other despising, his brother; and the mass of society is made up of morbid thinkers, and miserable workers. Now it is only by labour that thought can be made healthy, and only by thought that labour can be made happy, and the two cannot be separated with impunity. It would be well if all of us were good handicraftsmen in some kind, and the dishonour of manual labour done away with altogether.[17]

All men should be educated according to their capacity; and as for the ornamentist and his brother artists who sculpted and painted, it seemed to Ruskin that basically they were performing the same task. Therefore the oneness of their purpose and the dignity of their work made it imperative that they receive a similar education, and of the highest sort at that. Of the painters he once remarked, that one must try "to make, in the noble sense of the word, gentlemen of them; that is to say, to take care that their minds receive such training, that in all they paint they shall see and feel the noblest things."[18] True, he agreed with the system of teaching at South Kensington in so far as he felt no person was able to give "useful and definite help towards such special applications of art" as that of design, unless he were "entirely familiar with the conditions of labour and natures of material involved in the work";[19] but he felt this to be a secondary accomplishment to "be given in schools established by each trade for itself." His admonition to those engaged in educating designers for industry was this: "Try first to manufacture a Raphael; then let Raphael direct your manufacture."[20]

The utmost importance was thus assigned to the mental education of the artist, besides the development of his manual skill. Nature should constantly be kept before him; his material surroundings should be beautiful; the whole society in which he lived should breathe an atmosphere of kindness and peace. Ambition, for instance, Ruskin despised as a driving force for men's actions, and thought harmful because so often it leads to unkindness and to pride in social position: "The high ethical training of a nation implies perfect Grace, Pitifulness, and Peace; it is irreconcilably inconsistent ... with the desire of money,—and with mental states of anxiety."[21]

In many respects Ruskin ranks as the most important precursor of current ideas in modern social philosophy, which harks back to him through William Morris and the early Socialist movement; and in part his Utopia does not seem so very different from our own conception of the Welfare State. Maybe the main difference is that today materialist elements are stressed, while the basic idea of Ruskin's society was moral and aesthetic. We of today talk a great deal about the material standard of living, and in order to achieve it we have not as yet shown much hesitation in converting ploughed fields into aerodromes and befouling the air with industrial smoke. Maybe our towns are in some respects better today than they were in Ruskin's time a hundred years ago; still we are very far removed as yet from the image which he at that date ventured to paint of

lovely cities, crystallized, not coagulated, into form; limited in size, and not casting out the scum and scurf of them into an encircling eruption of shame, but girded each with its sacred pomoerium, and with garlands of gardens full of blossoming trees and softly guided streams—[22] .... The first schools of beauty must be the streets of your cities.[23]

The reader's thoughts inevitably glide to the mediaeval towns of Europe—the Italian, the French, the little ones of the Rhine valley; and it becomes evident how much in his dreams of what was to come Ruskin drew from his visions of the past.

The beauty—and the greatness—of Ruskin's thought becomes the more outstanding on deeper study; and only by extensive reading of his works do apparent paradoxes and contradictions resolve themselves, to be linked up naturally with the main body of his philosophy. It is true that frequently he irritates by his arrogance and by his one-track manner of reasoning; but then again, his humility is deep and sincere whenever shown, and if his attitude seems narrowly confined to his own line of thought, perhaps this is because his ideas so violently attack prejudices and conventions of our own daily life, maybe in themselves far more restricted, and certainly far less humanitarian. In the first part of this chapter I have tried to convey an understanding, sufficient for the present purpose, of the most fundamental ideas on which John Ruskin built his entire philosophy of art. For a study of the complexity and richness of this structure reference must be made to his own works; but even here most problems will resolve themselves, once the all-embracing principle of God-inspired nature and nature-inspired art has been grasped. Art is an expression of man's delight in the creation of God; it is there "to make you happy .... in looking at God; watching what He does; what He is; and obeying His law, and yielding yourself to His will."[24]—"All Art is Praise."[25]

This, then, is equally true of the major and the minor arts; and we have now arrived at the point where we must consider the latter, to find what forms, in Ruskin's opinion, should most appropriately be given them.

In his attitude to design Ruskin shared the predominating Victorian preference for associative ornament. He certainly understood the value of abstract design, but thought it so far inferior that in architecture he held sculpture and painting to be the chief features, and regretted the increasing tendency in architecture of his own day "to the prevalence of the lower part over the higher, to the interference of the constructive, with the purity and simplicity of the reflective, element."[26] This reflective element might be of a purely narrative character, or it might be expressive of forces and tensions in construction—as when Ruskin regretted, in the case of the new Battersea Bridge in London, the absence of grasping animal paws, or biting jaws to express the forces at work in the construction of the bridge where its cables and pavement join the banks on either side; and in architectural design as in every other kind he wanted first of all to see reflections of divinely inspired power and beauty of natural form.

Nature, however, should not be studied indiscriminately; certain forms have a higher value than others, and Ruskin thought himself

justified in considering those forms to be *most* natural which are most frequent; or, rather, that on the shapes which in the every-day world are familiar to the eyes of men, God has stamped those characters of beauty which He has made it man's nature to love.

In addition to this gradation he also introduced a hierarchy of forms, contending that "the noblest ornament" is that which represents "the highest orders of existence. Imitated flowers are nobler than imitated stones; imitated animals, than flowers; imitated human form, of all animal form the noblest."[27] In *Stones of Venice* a more elaborate list of precedence was given:

1. Abstract Lines
2. Forms of Earth (Crystals)
3. Forms of Water (Waves)
4. Forms of Fire (Flames and Rays)
5. Forms of Air (Clouds)
6. (Organic Forms) Shells
7. Fish
8. Reptiles and Insects
9. Vegetation (A). Stems and Trunks
10. Vegetation (B). Foliage
11. Birds
12. Mammalian animals and Man.

The author gravely defends the high position of vegetation, which he has put "apparently somewhat out of its place" because of "its vast importance as a means of decoration, and its constant association with birds and men,"[28] a fortunate circumstance which set it above reptiles and insects, not to mention fish and shells, as appropriate material for ornament.

This strange order of materials echoes the Christian conception of man as the flower of creation, and on the whole the order in which the various elements have been placed on the list bears considerable resemblance to the order in which according to the Bible they were created.

The list was compiled to show what sort of material was needed to form ornament of varying degrees of nobleness, according to what would be needed in each separate case; but however true to

nature, ornament must yet possess a second quality, without which
it is utterly base and useless:

the value of every work of art is exactly in the ratio of the quantity of
humanity which has been put into it, and legibly expressed upon it forever:
First, of thought and moral purpose; Secondly, of technical skill; Thirdly,
of bodily industry.[29]

From this, we may so far conclude about the character of Ruskinian
ornament, that it should be reminiscent of natural forms according
to an expressed order of precedence; and that it should show traces
of human effort, mental and physical.

It follows, then, that machine-made design must be bad, since •
there the second condition is not fulfilled; and "the absence of
the human labour ... makes the thing worthless."[30] Thus the industrial system of production became objectionable in yet another
sense; and all the mechanical aid which Ruskin deemed permissible
in the production of works of art was *"instruments which assist,
but do not supersede, the muscular action of the human hand."*[31]

We also possess from Ruskin's pen a few very interesting passages
which he evidently wrote prompted by the great interest in design
which the activities of Henry Cole and his collaborators had aroused;
they treat the problem of conventionalisation, for ornamental purposes, of natural form. The question had been raised at a meeting in 1856 between Ruskin and George Wallis, whom we recall as
an active member of the Schools of Design, and who was at this
time Headmaster of the Birmingham School of Art. Wallis had been
giving a lecture at the Society of Arts on "Recent Progress in Design
as applied to Manufacture", and complained that "the ladies especially, in spite of the best geometric designs, insist upon roses done in
wool." This being a blow at one of Ruskin's favourite principles,
he came to the defence of the fair sex:

He could not blame the ladies in this .... Nor could he see, since the first thing
we usually did to make the ground fit to be walked upon by any festive
procession, was always to strew flowers upon it, why we should refuse to have
flowers on our carpets, lest we should stumble over them.

In this he was of course in full agreement with little Sissy Jupe of *Hard Times*; but his next argument, that "he knew a most respectable and long-established firm, engaged in carpet manufacture on an extensive scale, which conducted its business on the principle Mr. Wallis opposed", does not indicate a very profound understanding of the aims of the Department. The same is true of his next remark, when he

referred to the firms whose head partners, the months of April and May, supplied a large part of the world with green carpets, in which floral design was largely introduced, and he believed generally to the satisfaction of the public.[32]

This same public, however, was probably a body that Ruskin would not have welcomed as a trustworthy judge of his own ideas, and it is surprising to find that he associated himself with it in condemning a different approach from his own to solve problems which were considered important to both parties. His criticism must be an outcome in this case of his general attitude of disapproval towards the basically commercial aims of his opponents.

Ruskin's views on the subject were set forth in *The Two Paths*, and I must beg my readers' pardon for making rather a long quotation from this source.

About the theorists at South Kensington he evidently felt that they made conventionalism too much an end in its own right. To Ruskin, it was nothing but a compromise, "*not* an improvement of natural form into something better or purer than Nature herself .... in all cases whatever, right conventionalism is either a wise acceptance of an inferior place, or a noble display of power under accepted limitation."[33]

He also heartily resented the separation between pictorial art and design as far as their respective formal manifestations were concerned, a principle which must be said to be implicit in the Department's aims and the entire conception of their mission. Ruskin's insistence on the oneness of art has been touched on before; to him, the only essential distinction between Decorative and other art is the being fitted for a fixed place; and in that place, related, either in subordination or in command, to the effect of other pieces of art....

The first order of it is that which is meant for places where it cannot be disturbed or injured, and where it can be perfectly seen; and then the main parts of it should be, and have always been made, by the great masters, as perfect, and as full of nature as possible.

You will every day hear it absurdly said that room decoration should be by flat patterns—by dead colours—by conventional monotonies, and I know not what. Now, just be assured of this—nobody ever yet used conventional art to decorate with, when he could do anything better, and knew that what he did would be safe .... And so in all other cases whatever, the greatest decorative art is wholly unconventional—downright, pure, good painting and sculpture, but always fitted for its place; and subordinated to the purpose it has to serve in that place.

So far, evidently, Ruskin was talking about higher forms of decorative art, like for instance architectural sculpture and painting. Descending yet another step, to objects of a less exalted character and more "liable to injury—to wear and tear; or to alteration of its form; as, for instance, on domestic utensils and armour, and weapons, and dress," he found that "forms of inferior art" would be needed,

such as will be by their simplicity less liable to injury: or, by reason of their complexity and continuousness, may show to advantage, however distorted by the folds they are cast into.

And thus arise the various forms of inferior decorative art, respecting which the general law is, that the lower the place and office of the thing, the less of natural or perfect form you should have in it; a zigzag or a chequer is thus a better, because a more consistent, ornament for a cup or platter than a landscape or portrait is: hence the general definition of the true forms of conventional ornament is, that they consist in the bestowal of as much beauty on the object as shall be consistent with its Material, its Place, and its Office.

This is not so different from Departmental principles after all, in spite of the difference between their respective points of departure. When it came to the process of conventionalisation itself, however, Ruskin recommended a "perfectly simple" principle which reduced all the careful ponderings of the South Kensington Art Department to nought: he admitted that the designer has "often to obtain beauty and display invention without direct representation of nature;" but feeling as he did, that "all noble ornamentation is the expression of Man's delight in God's work," he quite simply suggested, that

if the designer of furniture, of cups and vases, of dress patterns, and the like, exercises himself continually in the imitation of natural form in some leading division of his work; then, holding by this stem of life, he may pass down into all kinds of merely geometrical or formal design with perfect safety, and with noble results.[34]

Ruskin's theories of design in the strictest sense of the word, as understood by Henry Cole and his group, do not form any substantial part of his philosophy, and are of predominating interest not so much because they gave rise to any distinct school of ornament, as for their intimate relation to a revolutionary system of thought. The Ruskinian type of design would only be possible in a society completely different from any within the range of modern Western civilisation; and as the new realisation of these wider implications of his theories dawned upon him, Ruskin the Art Critic gradually developed into Ruskin the Social Reformer. There is a certain grim resolution about him in his latter capacity, as when he wrote that

I feel the force of mechanism and the fury of avaricious commerce to be at present so irresistible, that I have seceded from the study not only of architecture, but nearly of all art; and have given myself, as I would in a besieged city, to seek the best modes of getting bread and water for its multitudes, there remaining no question, it seems, to me, of other than such grave business for the time.[35]

Ruskin had many contemporary admirers, and his influence was tremendous throughout the Victorian era. Being himself a highly accomplished draughtsman, and a skilled water-colourist, he was felt to combine the knowledge of the scholar with the insight of the artist—a circumstance which gave added weight to his criticism of art. To my knowledge, however, no work exists to show that he exercised his talents as a designer. The best demonstration of his principles are therefore probably to be found in the Oxford Science Museum, which was erected in the 'fifties by the architect B. Woodward and at times closely supervised by Ruskin. The great writer was very interested in the scheme, and wanted the Museum to be something like a touchstone of his own ideas. The design, approaching 13th century Gothic, was supposed to unite the beautiful with the practical. In execution, material, etc., honesty and superior quality prevailed. Ruskin himself gave substantial sums for artistic embellishment, and made others join him to fulfil an elaborate scheme of decoration in painting and sculpture, although only parts of it were ever carried out. Among the workers were the famous O'Shea brothers, who carved decorative sculpture after flowers and plants from the Botanical Gardens in Oxford, and filled the arched doorway with parrots and owls of their own invention. In the great glass-roofed court, the pillars which carried the upper gallery and inner wall exhibited in their polished shafts a great variety of British rocks; in this way the very constructive members of the building were planned to be rich in associative and instructive value. Finally, the capitals give probably the best existing examples of what Ruskin himself considered as good design.

In *Fig. 15* I have given one from the lower arcade. Between the polished shaft and the lower part of polychrome arching the capital itself exhibits new and surprisingly unconventional features. Naturalistic leaves and flowers, every vein chiselled with care, are made to grow round the conic octagonal form of the capital, closely adapting themselves to its general outline; a diving bird adds complexity to the delicate design of bold undercutting and leaf-thin carving. There is no geometric pattern-making, and hardly any conventionalisation of detail forms; the only obvious adaptation to their special purpose which these plants have been made to undergo seems no more than the living leaves themselves might have been subjected to if carefully arranged by an expert florist. Such was the ideal which Ruskin opposed to the doctrinaires of the London Department.

HANDICRAFT, LEGEND, AND THE BEAUTY OF THE EARTH

William Morris

The names of John Ruskin and William Morris are frequently mentioned in the same breath, so intimate is the relation between them considered to be. And yet, with the younger of these two we enter upon a new stage in the history of 19th century design: Morris was the first among the Victorians to unite the talents of a designer with the executive skill of a craftsman. In this particular respect his example inspired a host of followers, who have mentioned his name with reverence right up to the present day.

Thus, in one sense Morris marked a new departure; yet his dependence on the older man is obvious. The entire philosophical background for his work in the arts was founded on Ruskin's ideas, and with these fresh in one's mind, most of Morris's thoughts on art and its relation to life will seem familiar. In the present context, therefore, all that is necessary is to stress outstanding points of difference and similarity so as to reach some estimate of the degree of Morris's dependence on his forerunner.

Born in 1834, he was Ruskin's junior by fifteen years, and so came under the influence of his works during the most formative period of his life, while up at Oxford from 1853. The chapter on

"The Nature of Gothic" from the second volume of *Stones of Venice* would be, he believed, in future times "considered as one of the very few necessary and inevitable utterances of the century"; towards the end of his life he wrote that "to some of us when we first read it, now many years ago, it seemed to point out a new road on which the world should travel".[1] This suggests of course the strong and lasting impression he received from this emphatic expression of Ruskin's central ideas; but it must not be thought that it was Ruskin who for the first time opened the young man's eyes to the miseries of the world: with Burne-Jones, his friend, he had long been intent upon a "holy crusade against the age", and the idea of some sort of "monastic" establishment, or a "brotherhood" of equal-minded friends, had already been nourished for some time when the writings of John Ruskin appeared on the scene. Through him Morris then learnt "to give form to my discontent, which I must say was not by any means vague", and it was largely through the agency of Ruskin that the leading passions in Morris's life became "the desire to produce beautiful things", and "hatred of modern civilization".[2]

The desire to produce beautiful things led in due time to the establishment of his firm, which came into being in 1861. It owed its existence not only to Ruskin, but to several friends from the Oxford days and from the circle of Pre-Raphaelite painters into which Morris and Burne-Jones had gained admittance in the middle fifties. It might be tempting to offer some suggestions as to the various influences which became manifest in this enterprise and in the products manufactured there—influences from men like Welby Pugin, or the Neo-Gothic architect William Butterfield, or Ford Madox Brown, the Pre-Raphaelite painter—or even from the writings and various activities of the Department of Science and Art. Without following up this question, I should none the less venture to suggest that the generally accepted notion of William Morris as the one and only reformer of taste in his day is strongly misleading. Ford Madox Brown had already claimed, for the furniture he designed, a place beside the paintings and sculpture which were exhibited by members of the Hogarth Club; and Rossetti had designed pieces of stained glass for one of the firms exhibiting in the Crystal Palace in 1851. The reformative activities of Pugin and of the men connected with the Department of Science and Art are also becoming gradually better known to us, and it does not seem at all unlikely that Morris himself may have known about them at an early date—despite his dislike of the Crystal Palace itself, which he is reported to have found "wonderfully ugly" and which he declined to enter when brought as a schoolboy to see it with his family. There also existed, in the person of his architect friend Philip Webb, a link with the rich tradition of the 'forties. Morris and Webb had both been articled to G. E. Street, the Gothic Revival architect, who was himself a pupil of Gilbert Scott, and at the same time strongly influenced by the far more artistically talented William Butterfield. "Red House", built in 1859 in Kent for Morris by Webb, and frequently accepted as revolutionary in its vaguely traditional, red-brick simplicity, most likely harks back through Street to straightforward, traditional and reasonably Gothic buildings like Butterfield's St. Saviour's Vicarage at Coalpitheath, built in the middle 'forties; and as for the use of unplastered brick, Pugin had employed yellow stocks at The Grange, 1841—43, and Philip Hardwick introduced frankly red-brick walls in his Hall and Library of Lincoln's Inn, London. These are only some among numerous examples quoted by Hitchcock in his recent work.

With regard, more specifically, to the Firm, its similarity to Pugin's workshops at Ramsgate has been suggested in an earlier chapter. But it would also be highly interesting if we could make clear to what extent the Firm exemplified Morris's own ideas of production in the crafts, and on what points it fell short. Peter Floud, in a study printed in *The Listener*, October 7th and 14th, 1954, throws some light on this question, and more may in due time be supplied through added research. In the present context the problem must unfortunately be left aside, so that our attention may be concentrated first on the relation, ideologically, between Morris and John Ruskin, next, on Morris's own specific theories of design.

Among the ideas of the older man, Morris seized firmly on the primary one that art can only grow out of happy work, and that happy work is not compatible with mechanical labour—or, at least, that higher forms of art cannot be produced by methods which largely supersede the actions of the human hand—that is with "more interposition of machines than is absolutely necessary to the nature of the work done."[3] All the same his hatred of monotonous labour was not unconditional, as is generally thought. For one thing, he found that "even mechanical labour is pleasant to some people (to me amongst others) if it be not too mechanical",[4] and in the general development of society as he saw it, he thought that "as an instrument for forcing on us better conditions of life" machinery "has been, and for some time yet will be, indispensable".[5] Even in his utopian conception of the future there would be a place kept for machines of a highly developed sort, to be "used freely for releasing people from the more mechanical and repulsive part of necessary labour"; for "it is the allowing machines to be our masters and not our servants that so injures the beauty of life nowadays—"[6] and only "as a condition of life, production by machinery is altogether an evil."[7]

Morris hoped for a return to a mental attitude which would make men like work, so that the aid of machines would not be wanted, because people would prefer the pleasure of exercising their own skill in the directest possible way:

we ought to get to understand the value of intelligent work, the work of men's hands guided by their brains, and to take that, though it be rough, rather than the unintelligent work of machines or slaves, though it be delicate; to refuse altogether to use machine-made work unless where the nature of the thing made compels it, or where the machine does what mere human suffering would otherwise have to do.[8]

This, of course, is entirely in line with Ruskin's opinions on the subject, and shows how Morris also borrowed from the older man the principles of limited consumption, holding that men's demands for goods ought to be regulated according to how the goods were produced, rejecting those produced at the cost of happiness in one form or another, and encouraging by increased demand the making of wares the production of which involved what he called pleasurable exercise of the human faculties. Morris was himself a man of refined but extremely simple tastes, and material luxury he felt was brought about by nothing but a "sickly discontent with the simple joys of the lovely earth".[9] A great many of the objects thought necessary for a happy middle-class life, he certainly managed to forgo; he would doubtless have managed without still more, if he could have had things his own way.

Artificiality or pretence of any sort he detested; he believed that a vast amount of pleasure lay ready at hand for anyone who would enter with interest into the daily and inevitable details of life, instead of pushing them off as mere nuisances, or hiding them away as offensive to good taste. He prided himself on being a good cook, and he got much genuine pleasure out of good food, good drink, good company, and working at his numerous crafts.[10] He was strong in his hatred against patterns of behaviour that distorted the free flow of human energies, and claimed what he once called "a free and unfettered animal life for man first of all". Going into further detail, he would

demand the utter extinction of all asceticism. If we feel the least degradation in being amorous, or merry, or hungry, or sleepy, we are so far bad animals, and therefore miserable men. And you know civilization *does* bid us to be ashamed of all these moods and deeds, and as far as she can, begs us to conceal them.[11]

It will be seen that despite the similarity of Ruskin's and Morris's insistence on the free exercise of human energies, there is a strong temperamental difference between them. Ruskin's idea of happiness was related to his belief in God, and he saw it as a partaking in the glory of Divine Creation. Morris, on the other hand, had assumed an agnostic attitude after his Oxford days, and his insistence on the "free and full life and the consciousness of life"[12] had nothing superhuman about it, since it was directed towards the exploitation—and, it should be said, refinement—of potential sources of happiness within the frame of inborn human capacities. Religion he feared, because it tended to impose patterns of behaviour in conflict with those dictated by human reason; he wanted to keep his future State "free of superstition", its ethics "based on the recognition of natural cause and effect, and not on rules derived from *a priori* ideas of the relation of man to the universe or some imagined ruler of it."[13] He desired "the least possible exercise of authority", and believed, in the words of his daughter, that

> by the time it is assumed that all men's needs must be satisfied according [to] the measure of the common wealth, what may be called the political side of the question would take care of itself ... [by adopting] a *public conscience* as a rule of action.[14]

This again runs counter to Ruskin, who had nourished ideas about some sort of aristocracy of the intellect to take the lead in his community of the future. As for Morris, the feeling for human fellowship was strong within him, and he wanted people to see that the main wrong in the existing system was

> the existence of class distinctions of any kind. I want there to be no more masters and slaves.... I want us all to be friends, all to be gentlemen, working for the common good, sharing duly the common stock of pleasure and refinement.[15]

Morris was looking forward to a Communist State; Ruskin had notions of a somewhat strictly organized aristocratic one; but both wanted people to be secure and happy, and believed that as far as art was concerned, its improvement would be impossible without extensive social reform. And Morris, most emphatically, insisted that current notions of culture and refinement were largely false: as he felt it, "simplicity of life, even the barest, is not a misery, but the very foundation of refinement."[16]

Together with Ruskin, Morris has been frequently accused of a wish to revert to mediaeval conditions of life; but, like the older man, his love for the Middle Ages—profound as it was—did not make him blind to the many points on which mediaeval life failed to conform to his own ideas of an ideal society. In *News from Nowhere*, Morris himself calls even the 19th century "a great improvement" on "the Mediaeval period, and the ferocity of its criminal laws," and on the ways in which "in those days men fairly seemed to have enjoyed tormenting their fellow men."[17] But what he *did* admire in those past times was the way in which (to him) beauty seemed to have grown out of everything they did, and how, in spite of tyrannical oppression, he could not "help thinking that sorely as poor folks needed a solace, they did not altogether lack one, and that solace was pleasure in their work."[18] Because he set such high store by this particular advantage, he even said once that "the Middle Ages, so to say, saw the promised land of Socialism from afar," and he believed that those times had in them the true foundations of a happy communal order if only "the leading element of association in the life of the mediaeval workman could have cleared itself of certain drawbacks;" with this he was thinking of the development of guild organisation, which ended by being an instrument for political and economic exploitation on the part of the upper classes.[19] However, as his conception of history was an evolutionistic one, he looked with confidence to the future; his was the belief that "all the change and stir about us is a sign of the world's life, and that it will lead—by ways, indeed, of which we have no guess—to the bettering of all mankind."[20] With this hope before him, he could decide to "choke down the sad sentiments" which, he admitted, "it is natural to feel over the death of the past,"[21] and to work for the bettering of a future world.

"An idle singer of an empty day" is the description which Morris gave of himself in one of his early poems; it is certainly without any meaning when applied to his later years. Yet his early days were active enough, building himself an extraordinary house, writing poetry, studying art, managing the Firm. Then, in 1876,[22] he started his life as a public figure by becoming Treasurer of the Eastern Question Association, and taking part in the Anti-Turk campaign as a Liberal. In the following years his development of ideas in politics and art may be traced through his activities in the Society for the Protection of Ancient Buildings (from 1877), in the Social Democratic Federation which he joined in 1883 after breaking with the Liberals, in the Socialist League (from 1885), and in the Hammersmith Socialist Society (from 1890). The writings of this period include his editorship of *Justice*, the organ of the Democratic Federation, and of the *Commonweal*, mouthpiece of the Socialist League. Among his socialistic writings are numerous songs, articles, and lectures, *A Dream of John Ball* (1888), and the utopian *News from Nowhere* (1891). Other literary works included the publication of lectures under the title of *Hopes and Fears for Art* (1882), various prose-romances, a translation of the Odyssey, and *Socialism, its Growth and Outcome*, written jointly with Belfort Bax (1893). Neither his Firm nor any of these were doings of an idle singer, and there have been few men whose days have been less empty than those of William Morris.

With respect to the future for which he worked—whatever it might turn into, he felt secure that art would have its place in it; and even if he dared not say what forms that art would assume, he felt equally confident that it would be the property of all, forming a part of the life of every man, his dress, his furniture, his house and his country. For to Morris art was not a thing to be restricted within the frame of a picture and stuck on the wall, but a force allied to the very urge for life itself—something like a fundamental will to harmony, health , and beauty. Therefore, his concern was not primarily with books, or paintings, or architecture, or politics, or even design: his themes were "The Beauty of Life" and "Art and the Beauty of the Earth".[23]

The development of the Morris firm ran parallel to his other activities, and its main steps may be recapitulated by the following dates:[24] it was founded in 1861, its production comprising cabinet-making, tile-painting, and stained glass, with table-glass designed by Philip Webb, the architect who was William Morris's friend and built his house. Paper-hangings were added in 1862, *Trellis* and *Daisy* being the first designs. In 1865 the business was moved from 8, Red Lion Square to Queen Square, where Morris came to live above the workshops. Then followed a series of commissions which helped considerably in bringing the names of the Firm and its owner before the public: The Green Dining-Room at South Kensington Museum was decorated in 1867; in 1870–72 decorative works were carried out at Peterhouse, Cambridge; in 1880 the Firm obtained the commission for decorating the throne-room at St. James's Palace. In the meantime the original partnership had been broken up and the Firm left entirely in Morris's care in 1875; two years afterwards showrooms were opened in Oxford Street. Then, in 1881 the whole workshop was again moved, this time to Merton Abbey at Hammersmith, and that same year two new important features were introduced into the production—the Morris Chintzes and tapestry weaving. The first large tapestry figure-piece was called the Goose-Girl and was designed by Walter Crane.

Mackail gives a list of all the kinds of work designed and executed at Hammersmith:

1. Painted glass windows.
2. Arras tapestry woven in the high-warp loom.
3. Carpets.
4. Embroidery.
5. Tiles.
6. Furniture.
7. General house decorations.
8. Printed cotton goods.
9. Paper hangings.
10. Figured woven stuffs.
11. Furniture velvets and cloths.
12. Upholstery.[25]

Thus, by the beginning of the 'eighties the Firm had settled into its final shape, producing a wide range of art goods; at that same period Morris's interest took a serious and decidedly political turn, which lasted with undiminished force through the whole decade. Then the beginning of the next decade saw a reversion to literature and the arts, marked by the establishment of the Kelmscott Press in 1890.

It will be seen that Morris had a long career behind him as an artist, poet, and writer, before he started to formulate his views on art: his first effort in this direction was a lecture on "The Decorative Arts", delivered in 1877. It was the first he ever gave, and was followed by a steady stream of others dealing increasingly with art in its social implications, as their author's interests swung in the direction of politics and questions of communal welfare. A considerable part of these lectures have a more or less direct bearing on design, and it is to them we shall have to turn for our present investigations into the views Morris held on his own craft.

Acquaintance with the works of William Morris is an enchanting experience, which makes it transparently clear what a born artist in design he was. Within its own limitations the genuine William Morris product shows a depth of feeling and richness of imagination scarcely surpassed, I venture to say, by artists of any time; in it he combined what can best be described as a tactile feeling for material with exquisite perception of colour. He also had an inborn capacity for making his designs flow and develop with freedom and ease, fullbodied and mature, in masterly compositions kept in effortless balance. It will be seen that this description is one best applied to design in flat pattern; it is, however, applicable to all Morris's work, because it is doubtful whether he may be classed as a designer of three-dimensional objects at all. There is the story of the heavy carpentry furniture at Red Lion Square in the 'fifties, which seems mostly to have been designed from hasty sketches in order to provide spacious panels for painted pictorial decoration. The widely known rush-seated chairs produced by the Firm were adapted from models found on farms in Sussex, and the adjustable padded arm-chair, the

"Morris chair", was evidently designed by Warrington Taylor;[26] and Morris himself,

with the exception of a few very early pieces for his own use.... appears never to have designed furniture (despite frequent statements to the contrary), or any other three-dimensional object in pottery or metal.[27]

Morris's preoccupation with flat-pattern design—and most of all with textiles—may have been a result of his all-overpowering love for associative matter in design, which in this connection became satisfied, in most cases, by suggesting a background in natural beauty. With the unimportant exception of the early furniture at Red Lion Square, his connection with the design of furniture was so far as we know as a painter of legends or stories on the panels of it—as on the cabinet in *Fig. 16*, or on another cabinet designed by the architect J. P. Seddon for himself, but made and decorated by the Firm.[28] Many of Morris's textiles have figures and inscriptions on them, and he never designed anything purely abstract that had not a clear relation to forms in nature: even where his designs included nothing but flowers and leaves he never intended them to be void of meaning. Speaking of pattern-designing, he said that "without meaning, it were better not to exist."[29] There should be "a certain mystery" in it, and we should

clothe our daily and domestic walls with ornament that reminds us of the outward face of the earth, of the innocent love of animals, or of man passing his days between work and rest as he does.[30]

He believed this love for a story to be typical of Western art, and he even went so far as to call Eastern art "to a certain extent, the uncivilized",[31] because there this tendency was less marked. Of himself he said that

I, as a Western man and a picture-lover, must still insist on plenty of meaning in your patterns; I must have unmistakable suggestions of gardens and fields, and strange trees, boughs, and tendrils, or I can't do with your pattern.[32]

In this he was of course very close to Ruskin, and like him, he talks of a separation between *architecture* and *building*, and defined the former as "the art of ornamental building";[33] as for the designer, his teachers "must be Nature and History".[34] The difference between the two, however, is also evident: for where Ruskin saw design as an interpretation of God in nature, Morris the agnostic loved it for its own sake, irrespective of any associations of divinity, and his enchanting ability to convey the sense of wonder and loving amazement which he himself felt in the face of nature and history and the legends of man, is what will always mark him as a designer not of the brain, but of rich phantasy and of the heart. All the same, his was a talent that never overstepped the limits of Victorian interest in symbolism and narration of one form or another; therefore, to the modern movement towards abstract and non-representational forms of beauty in design he contributed nothing.

It is very doubtful whether Morris ever held theory as such in anything but low esteem, as a necessity of evil conditions—born artist as he was, and endowed, as he himself said, with a constructive rather than an analytical mind.[35] He definitely held that doing was better than talking, and believed that "when people talk most about Works of Art, generally speaking at that period they do least in art;"[36] his own writings and lectures on the subject are more concerned with how to create conditions for art to grow than how to create the forms of that art. This was to him a matter of feeling more than of theory.

As to educating designers, he believed in developing their natural abilities through teaching drawing, preferably of the human figure; drawing in general would also increase knowledge of nature, since only natural objects would serve as fit models for exercise. As to the Schools of Design, Morris said that he

did not under-value the importance of these places of instruction; on the contrary, I believe them to be necessary to us, unless we are prepared to give up all attempt to unite these two elements of use and beauty.

Further he said,

I do not think any reasonable man can consider them a failure when the condition of the ornamental part of the individual arts is considered at the time of their foundation. True it is that those who established them were partly influenced by a delusive expectation that they would presently be able to supply directly a demand which was felt for trained and skilful designers of goods; but, though this hope failed them, they have no doubt influenced both that side of art and others also; among all that they have done not the least is that public recognition of the value of art in general which their very existence implies.

As for the principles of design formulated "at the very first foundation of these schools [by] the instructors in them", he found that they were formulated "clearly and satisfactorily", and thought "they have since been accepted generally, at least in theory".[37] Thus he was clearly well informed about those early efforts, and this gives reason to believe, when we meet similarities of views held by the early pioneers and himself, that Morris may in some measure have adopted such of their principles as he found of use to him. But the entire system for the improvement of which the schools worked was distasteful to him; and the work of a modern industrial designer he rather thought of

in this fashion: that a highly gifted and carefully educated man shall, like Mr. Pecksniff, squint a sheet of paper, and that the results of that squint shall set a vast number of well-fed, contented operatives.... turning crank handles for ten hours a-day—[38]

which, of course, was hardly a vision to conform to his own bold idea of "an *art which is to be made by the people and for the people, as a happiness to the maker and the user*".[39]

To pass from the designer to design itself Morris deeply distrusted any "scientific" approach: "the royal road of a set of rules deduced from a sham science of design, that is itself not a science but another set of rules, will lead nowhere," and "*designing* cannot be taught at all in a school". A school can give designers certain technical knowledge, "just as they want tools", and in the prevailing low standard of practice "they do undoubtedly want instruction in the history of the arts".[40] Good drawing is also necessary, but the capacity for designing would still not lie in any of these, but in the designer's own feeling for his work.

It has already been mentioned that Morris found a certain difference in temperament between Eastern and Western design. This was not only manifested in the different attitude to the narrative part of it, but also in the manner in which models from nature were to be conventionalised to make up a good pattern. There are, of course, first the various modes of building up a skeleton for recurring surface-pattern—the one with which Morris himself was most frequently occupied—and he mentions the basic constructive schemes of

(1) Horizontal stripes; (2) block diaper or chequer; (3) matting diaper, very various in form; (4) square line diaper; (5) floriated square diaper; (6) round diaper formed by contiguous circles; (7) the diagonal branch; (8) the net; (9, which is supplementary) powderings on the lines of the diagonal branch, or of the net.

But these basic forms must be "clothed with flesh, that is, their members must have tangible superficial area",[41] and this is where the two different attitudes show themselves. The Western mind, strongly bent on expressing itself through form, prefers to work in light colour upon a dark ground; thus, Morris contended, "there is often an impression given, of there being more than one plane in the pattern. Where the pattern is strictly on one plane, we have not reached the full development of this manner of designing", which is "the full development of colour and form used together, but form predominant". This, then, was the

Western and civilized method: that used by craftsmen who were always seeing pictures, and whose minds were full of definite ideas of form. Colour was essential to their work, and they loved it and understood it, but always subordinated it to form.[42]

We see how this assertion was true of Morris's own work, if we look at the design for a "Blackthorn" wallpaper in *Fig 17*. This design has a clearly defined depth into which the floral forms recede in their intertwining movement; but each single member is clearly defined, while still being kept in perfect relation to the general scheme of development.

The Eastern attitude to design was one which, in the way it

handled its elements, ultimately led to a pattern where the chief interest was in planes of colour carefully balanced into harmony, and separated each by a line of another colour;

which outlining, while it serves the purpose of gradation, which in more naturalistic work is got by shading, makes the design quite flat, and takes from it any idea of there being more than one plane in it.

This method Morris called "the Eastern, and, to a certain extent, the uncivilized", because of its inferior capacity for narrative elements in one form or another. True enough, works produced in this manner as "found in Persian art at its best, do carry the art of mere pattern-designing to its utmost perfection, and it seems somewhat hard to call such an art uncivilized;" but its failure, however glorious, consisted in paying more attention to artistic elements for their own sake, than for the sake of the meaning they convey; for Morris was convinced that "colour for colour's sake only will never take real hold on the art of our civilization, not even in its subsidiary art"; and "to have a meaning and to make others feel and understand it, must ever be the aim and end of our Western art". Indeed, Morris called "meaning" a "moral" quality of design, probably because it revealed the designer's attitude to the world around him.

In Morris's observation on Eastern design—planes of colour bounded by lines of a different colour—we find a parallel to suggestions for managing colour in Jones's proposition 29, 30, 31, 32, and 34; but in his more subtle conception of depth in pattern-design, Morris was able to disregard his predecessor's insistence on unconditional flatness. It may also be said as a very general observation that, where Jones's patterns may give a somewhat starved impression of having obtained this flatness through some kind of *papier collage* method, Morris's forms seem almost to pulsate and grow with slow movement in a foreground space of a certain depth, which confines their growth, but does not affect the life of it.

Though he was clearly a born designer, it will of course all the same be understood that Morris gave much thought to the principles of an art which he seemingly mastered with such ease and completeness; but as we have seen him despise what he called the "sham science of design", his advice, when he gave it, took the form of general observations rather than definite rules.

The necessity for conventionalisation of forms was "in theory .. accepted everywhere", and what he chiefly had to say about it was "that it does not excuse want of observation of nature, or laziness of drawing, as some people seem to think." Good conventional design, to "fill a space properly, or look crisp and sharp", must be built on solid knowledge of natural form; and from this it follows "that your convention must be your own, and not borrowed from other times and peoples".

Apart from the general limitations imposed upon the artist by formal treatment, Morris also points to the more particular ones of use and material and modes of production, "generally unheeded at present"; but in mastering his material, overcoming its difficulties, and making the most of its facilities, the thoughtful designer also knows where to stop. He must forgo any attempt "to make people stare" at his "dexterity in dealing with a difficult thing", and so convert art into a mere toy and himself into "a juggler". Contrariwise he urges

try to get the most out of your material, but always in such a way as honours it most. Not only should it be obvious what your material is, but something should be done with it which is specially natural to it, something that could not be done with any other.[43]

He says of wallpaper design that it is "a cheap art, somewhat easily done; elaborate patterns are easy in it; so be careful not to overdo either the elaboration in your paper or the amount of pattern-work in your rooms." Also, in such a very mechanical process, the imitation of natural form should be least direct, while at the same time the construction of pattern must be masked with more than ordinary care, in order not to be obtrusive in these wares made to be "stretched out flat on the wall" and without any "special beauty of execution about them". What has to be done to meet the difficulties of designing for printed paper-hangings, is to create due paper-stainers' flowers and leaves, forms that are obviously fit for printing with a block; to mask the construction of our pattern enough to prevent people from counting the repeats of our pattern, while we manage to lull their curiosity to trace it out; to be careful to cover our ground equably. If we are successful in these two last things, we shall attain a look of satisfying mystery, which is an essential in all patterned goods, and which in paperhangings must be done by the designer, since, as aforesaid, they fall into no folds, and have no special beauty of material to attract the eye.

Above all things the colour should be very modest since the material is commonplace and the manufacture mechanical; at all cost, "no colour should ever be muddy or dingy."[44] This was what most of all offended Morris's own very fine perception of this side of his art. It should, however, be noted that in spite of the great popularity of his own designs in this material, Morris thought wallpapers but poor makeshifts, and preferred pure whitewash in most cases.

Design for cotton-printing comes in much the same category as wallpaper design, only that here construction of pattern has not necessarily to be masked so carefully, because the material is bound to "fall into folds, or turn round furniture"; in addition, the charm of printed cotton is enhanced by the dyes, which if genuine have "always some beauty of their own".

The same consideration as to construction is relevant in the case of figured woven stuffs, in which, however, the material and technique impose more severe limitations upon the designer—who for that reason "will not be so much beset by the dangers of commonplace" and "cannot choose but make [his] ... flowers weaver's flowers". But the art being a nobler one than that of paper-staining and cotton-printing, "it claims from us a higher and more dignified style of design. Your form must be clearer and sharper, your drawing more exquisite, your pattern must have more of meaning and history in it." And in this product even more beauty should be obtained from the material itself than was the case with printed cottons.

As for carpet-design, "it seems quite clear that it should be quite flat, that it should give no more at least than the merest hint of one plane behind another." And this was not on the ground that a three-dimensional carpet-design would offend our reason, or deceive our imagination into creating a fear of stumbling—as had been the argument of Pugin and the Reformers in the Schools of Design; Morris's objection was purely artistic—that

every little bit of surface must have its own individual beauty of material and colour .... Now, if in our coarse, worsted mosaic we make awkward attempts at shading and softening tint into tint, we shall dirty our colour and so degrade our material.

Therefore the method most appropriate is the one which he had earlier called the Eastern manner of surrounding

all or most of your figure by a line of another tint .... If this is well done, your pieces of colour will look gemlike and beautiful in themselves, your flowers will be due carpet-flowers, and the effect of the whole will be soft and pleasing;

but precedent for this has probably to be got from the school of Eastern designers, "as this in its perfection is a speciality of theirs".

Pottery-painting he held to be a difficult craft, because the danger here of falling into "sham naturalistic platitude" is very great, "since we have no longer to stamp our designs with a rough wood-block on paper or cotton, ... but, pencil in hand, may do pretty much what we will." However, the limitation first to be remembered is that of the space allotted by the form of the object so to be decorated; and as to the instrument which is used for this art—"a long, sharp-pointed brush charged with heavy colour"—it offers peculiar possibilities for characteristic design when used "with a firm, deliberate, and decided, but speedy hand".

Design for embroidery Morris considered to stand "midway between that for tapestry and that for carpets"; but as its technical limits were less severe, it "is very apt to lead people into cheap and commonplace naturalism"; this danger would be best avoided by remembering

that our roses and the like, however unmistakably roses, shall be quaint and naïve to the last degree, and also, since we are using specially beautiful materials, that we shall make the most of them, and not forget that we are gardening with silk and gold-thread.

Since this art is one of pure luxury, he urges that special care should be taken to ensure that it be beautiful—or it will all be made in vain.

In embroidery as in other products for which Morris was responsible, colour always plays an important part in contributing to the general effect. His eye for colour was extremely sensitive, and for purposes of dyeing and wherever else they could be used, he preferred vegetable colours—detesting above all the chemical aniline dyes which so drastically changed the look of Victorian textiles when they were introduced in the 'forties. Morris's own experiments to improve the colours used by the Firm are well known, and doubtless he was responsible for preserving much knowledge which has later been put to use by studio craftsmen in many countries. Apart from mere technicalities connected with their use, however, he said prudently enough that "one can only give warnings against possible faults; it is clearly impossible to teach colour by words"— though teaching in a workshop would be effective, at least partially. His own general advice was to "be rather restrained than over-luxurious in colour", to be "frank and simple", and not attempt "over-refinements".[45] His views on the relationship between colour and form in design have already been mentioned, together with the deeper significance he assigned to it.

Detailed notes on the use of colour for particular purposes are few, but where they occur he seems to have been guided more by intuitive feeling than by consideration of very definite rules. One would believe that he was well read in the subject, and knew the order of colour built on the three primaries; but here again, scientific knowledge does not seem to have crystallized into definite rules, as it tended to do, for instance, in the far more systematic principles of Owen Jones; and when speaking, as in one case he did, of distempered wall-decoration, he simply gave a list of favourite colours, with some personal comments; in the list are,

a solid red, not very deep, but rather describable as a full pink, and toned both with yellow and blue, a very fine colour if you can hit it. A light orangy pink, to be used rather sparingly. A pale golden tint, *i. e.*, a yellowish-

brown; a very difficult colour to hit. A colour between these two last; call it pale copper colour. All these three you must be careful over, for if you get them muddy or dirty you are lost.
Tints of green from pure and pale to deepish and grey: always remembering that the purer the paler, and the deeper the greyer.

And so on. Green he calls "a work-a-day colour", blue "the holiday one". As to his own genuine feeling for the qualities of all of them, his work testifies better than descriptions.

Considering general qualities of design, Morris insisted upon a feeling of consistency and completeness about a pattern. The ground must be covered "equally and richly", and "every line in a pattern should have its due growth", and "be traceable to its beginning . . . . Mutual support and unceasing progress distinguish real and natural order from its mockery, pedantic tyranny."[46] And for details as well as bigger parts, "above all things, avoid vagueness; . . . Definite form bounded by firm outline is a necessity for all ornament."[47]

Into Morris's own highly personal patterns were woven influences from many sources—indicative of the extensive study of mediaeval textiles of Sicily, of the woven patterns of the near East, of Elizabethan and 17th century English design. Some of his works bear considerable relation to prototypes like these, while others show an entirely fresh and personal approach to an age-old field of art, and became themselves sources of inspiration for subsequent craftsmen.

As an example of William Morris's design at its best, I have chosen the embroidery in *Fig. 18*—a wall-hanging done in wool on linen, designed about 1880, and probably worked by Margaret Bell (wife of Sir Lowthian Bell).[48] Here is complete balance between the main parts of panel and border; the main divisions of the panel, showing somewhat less emphatically in the original, give a firm basic structure; between them the rich and varied growth of leaves and flowers is distributed on the ground sufficiently sparsely to allow the coarse linen to give its contrast of rougher texture to the soft and softly-coloured wool. The forms are conventionalised and firmly restrained within the space allotted to each part; even so there is scarcely any stiffness about them, although they are "quaint and naïve" enough, and crisp also. An outer wave-line border, and two inner ones—a dog-tooth one and another resembling a twisted rope-border—are the only non-representational parts of the design. Everything else is made up of natural form, adapted to a degree of flatness appropriate to the purpose, but not crushed into one plane: they seem to move slightly in depth. There is no hint at stylistic copyism in this design; it breathes a freshness and purity completely free from sophistication, and shows a delicacy in harmony of colours beyond that dictated by cold principle. It proves Morris—as indeed his undogmatic principles also do—"the fertile man, he of resources," whose work "will grow on and on, one thing leading to another, as it fares with a beautiful tree".[49]

He was an artist who worked in full sympathy with his craft, and loved it.

With regard to furniture and interior decoration in general, it has been made clear that Morris was himself making designs for only special parts of it; which did not prevent his having his likes and dislikes when considering the general scheme. His taste was set on simplicity in this as in most other matters. Simplicity, however, would not mean meagreness, since "if we really care for art we shall always feel inclined to save on superfluities, that we may have a wherewithal to spend on works of art." Thus, he wanted his furniture to be soundly constructed "on the proper principles of the art of joinery", and "except for very moveable things like chairs" he wanted some substance in his pieces: "it should be made of timber rather than walking-sticks". But first of all there should be no more furniture in a room than what was really needed for daily use: shelves for books, chairs and seats to sit on, tables to eat or write at. And besides these articles of "work-a-day furniture", "simple to the last degree", there would still be room for another kind, which Morris called "state-furniture", and which he thought "proper even for a citizen; I mean sideboards, cabinets, and the like, which we have quite as much for beauty's sake as for use." On these, no pain and trouble should be spared to gain richness and beauty by carving, inlaying, and painting, for "these are the blossoms of the art of furniture", which should not be scattered haphazardly about the house, but "used architecturally to dignify important chambers and important places in them."[50]

The cabinet in *Fig. 16*, with its choice materials and costly painting, would be an example of what Morris meant by state-furniture; another example is given by the escritoire in *Fig. 19*, from the Firm's later days. The older one, heavily mediaeval, was designed by Philip Webb in 1861, and represented the Firm in the World Exhibition the year after. It shows how intimate was the relation of the Morris circle in its early days to the spirit of the Gothic Revival; but frank mediaevalism has not prevented the piece from being built soundly, if somewhat heavily, on constructive principles and from also being well adapted to its purpose. Its supreme beauty in the eyes of the young artists themselves must however be supposed to rest in the pictorial scenes from the legend of St. George which Morris himself painted on the panels. This kind of painted furniture is, I believe, so far unique in the history of the 19th century; but in its bearing on the present subject, it is a practice which more than anything seems to show how strongly steeped the newly-founded Firm was in the love of story-telling which had so far manifested itself in most Victorian design, in one way or another.

The cabinet made in the Firm's later years, elegant almost to sophistication, was designed by the American architect-designer George Jack, in 1893, after he had been chief furniture-designer to Morris & Co. for about three years. In style it seems to be somewhat influenced by Japanese and Chinese furniture—the box-like upper part, the angular feet, and the somewhat abrupt profile of the longitudinal member forming part of the strengthening frame between the legs, point in this direction; the material is also exotic—marquetry of sycamore and various woods. The decoration, on the other hand, strikes a familiar note with its homely growth of oak and ash and coltsfoot arranged in formal and yet lively pattern. But the supreme hand of the master himself can scarcely be supposed to have a part in a design where these have been joined by a set of thin and dry lines crossing each other in chequers on the top. The workmanship, however, is superb, and the result a costly and elegant, yet beautiful and functional simplicity. Luxuriousness—yes; but permitted luxury, "if it be done for beauty's sake, and not for show". It did not break Morris's golden rule, which set the standard for all his opinions on this matter—have nothing "for mere finery's sake, or to satisfy the claim of custom;"[51] and above all, *have nothing in your houses which you do not know to be useful or believe to be beautiful."*[52]

It is probably not easy to over-estimate the position of William Morris among the designers and craftsmen of the Victorian era. He certainly did not stand alone—the name of an artist like Welby Pugin looms large, and the activities as well as the theories of those connected with Henry Cole and the various Governmental establishments for the improvement of design have been of importance even, as it may be suggested, to William Morris himself. Yet, his was the more richly varied genius. It sought expression in verse and in prose, as well as in design and through an absolutely fabulous manual dexterity in handling the most varied of crafts and materials. His most outstanding achievement was probably this, that in an age when manual labour and purely executive skill were despised by the upper classes, he, on the strength of his works and his reputation as a poet, forced through a new respect for hand and brain working together. By exemplifying in his own life the ideal of the craftsman, he carried the most central ideas of John Ruskin into life, at the same time pointing, in his principles of labour and workshop organisation, to an alternative to the solution sought by official bodies for problems concerning art-manufacture and design. The studio craftsman of our day is a direct outcome of an example set by Morris himself; in other ways too, but not least through this kind of artist,

Morris's influence on the products of modern mechanised industry has been immense. He was himself a great artistic genius, to be remembered not only for what he preached, but for what he himself produced.

He did not overthrow the supremacy of modern industry, as he wanted to; but within the new order of things he enforced respect for the hand-made product, and secured the recognition, beside the machine, of the individual artist-craftsman.

AESTHETICISM, SYMBOLIC ORNAMENT, AND FUNCTIONAL FORM

E. W. Godwin, The Arts and Crafts, and Christopher Dresser

In his career and in his work William Morris gave life to the teachings of John Ruskin, and struck out a new road for designers in his own day and after. The theories on various aspects of his craft which he expounded do not, however, stand alone; but they are the best known, and the most prominent among other efforts in a similar direction during the time. His name became illustrious because of the splendour of his art, and because he infused life into the idea that man should attain to happiness and mental health through striving for beauty.

This legacy from Ruskin was also taken up by others, most of them also influenced by Morris's work and writings, some few acting in independence of him.

Among the latter, the architect *Edward William Godwin*[1] is the most outstanding figure; active in the 'sixties and 'seventies, he was the one who brought the most exciting and personal artistic gifts to bear on his work. His writings are few and insignificant, so that his importance rests on his being a designer always on the radical side, and well-known to the public; young admirers of the late 'sixties pronounced him the most excellent designer of the day.

He started his career as a promising Neo-Gothic architect, building Northampton Town Hall between 1860 and 1864. He received advice on it from Ruskin, and organized a team of workmen on much the same lines as the latter had attempted to do during the building of the new museum at Oxford. On the whole, Godwin was very much taken by Ruskin's ideas about life being integrated with art, and worked towards free artistic creation on the principle of utility combined with beauty. He was probably the strongest exponent in England of an influence springing from Japanese art, which he studied as early as 1860; later his house in Bristol was decorated internally with painted walls, Japanese prints, Persian rugs, antique furniture carefully selected—and for this "there was no contemporary precedent".[2]

Godwin saw art as a unity and claimed for the architect the right to design furniture and interior decorations. His career as a commercial designer, working outside the frame of architectural commissions, started in 1868, when he designed a coffee-table in ebonised wood for William Watt *(Fig. 20)*[3]; in this and in later work of his there is an effort towards lightness and serviceableness, combined with carefully calculated balance of colour and form. In this respect Godwin was much attracted by Japanese art because of its careful planning of aesthetic effect and its light, constructive character; and he employed Japanese designs in decorative plaques and in wallpapers because of their highly decorative, flat-pattern qualities. When his early furniture became too costly, he eventually designed some cheaper pieces, not particularly modern, but of a utilitarian character to meet public demand.[4]

Always a radical on architectural questions, he applauded Norman Shaw's introduction of the Queen Anne style in 170, Queen's Gate, London; he held it a step in the direction of greater simplicity and economy in architectural design; and a year after its erection, he wrote that "The day of architectural revivals may be setting—I for one sincerely hope it is."[5] The house he built for Whistler in Chelsea in 1877, "White House", marked an effort to reduce architecture to bare essentials. All formal convention was sacrificed to convenience, and the architectural composition of facade made subject to interior planning so that windows were placed where they were needed, and not where symmetry told them to go. In its lack of exterior ornament this house was extreme—indeed so much so that the local building authorities enforced the application of some ornamental stucco plaques; but these were made in very plain material, as Whistler had planned to have them knocked off later. The house caused a considerable stir in artistic circles, and is remarkable as an example of functionalism at a very early date.

Godwin had wide connections with artists and people of the stage, and he did a great deal to reform stage-design in England—working successfully even at the art of staging itself. His importance for the Aesthetic Movement of the 'seventies and 'eighties has always been fully recognized; he saw in it a possibility for a general cultivation of taste, and an encouragement of a fresh and unconventional approach to life. The aesthetes, who were attracted by the artistic charm of Japan and William Morris, the idealism and art-life theory of Ruskin, the mysticism of Swinburne, the elegance of Wilde, and the free treatment of artistic means of expression practised by Whistler—the aesthetes as a group were probably guilty of mannerisms and affectations which made them deserve the laughter of *Punch*, and the ridicule of Gilbert and Sullivan; but in spite of everything that might be said against them, there can hardly be any doubt that they did much to promote a general interest in art and design; and it is very probable that Godwin expressed their mutual aspiration towards a life of beauty, when in his short booklet on *Dress* he wrote,

to commit beauty— because we cannot help it; to make for the healthy—as a matter of course; to breathe in an atmosphere where the sunbeam throbs with art, and the rain is woven with sanitation, are, perhaps, possible only in the land of Utopia. We might, however, make for that land, and near it... by that old Japanesy method of taking delight in all that contributes to beauty and health.[6]

Godwin began his career when William Morris was yet without any considerable influence, and little known by the general public. His achievement was of a highly personal kind, and would merit a far more thorough treatment in a study of a nature less theoretical than the present one. We know nothing about a possible relation between him and William Morris, although it is far from unlikely that they may have been in touch with one another;[7] ideally at any rate they belong together, because of their common root in the teachings of Ruskin, and because of their longing for some sort of social life where art would form an integral part.

Another very influential writer who also belongs to the eighteen-sixties, and shared with Morris and Godwin a common background in the Gothic Revival, and to a less marked extent in the teachings of John Ruskin, was the architect *Charles L. Eastlake*, nephew of Sir Charles, the painter, and famous as the contemporary chronicler of the 19th century Gothic Revival. His book *Hints on Household Taste* was published in 1868, the major part of its contents having appeared as a series of articles from 1864; the book ran to four London and six New York editions, and was at that date probably quite as important an influence as William Morris, addressing itself as it did to the general public, to show "how they may furnish their houses with a sense of the picturesque which shall not interfere with modern notions of comfort and convenience".[8] Eastlake advocated a somewhat sturdy, rustic style, uncomfortable, but marked by good honest carpentry and a will for simplicity and cleanliness; he had earlier blamed Morris's Firm for its heavy and expensively painted furniture, because an article of that sort "ought to be artistic *in itself*, and produced at a price which the general public will pay, before we call in the painter's aid to please those who can afford a luxury."[9]

Edward Godwin and Charles Eastlake are the most prominent of those architects, craftsmen, and designers who in the 'sixties expounded the theory of design in a more or less close relation to John Ruskin's views; Morris, it must be remembered, was as yet only a workshop manager and a craftsman who was gradually attracting notice by his outstanding ability. His writings on theory belong to the time between the late 'seventies and his death in 1896.

To them, however, and to the work and personality of their author as a whole, should be attributed the influence which in the 'eighties brought to life a series of craftsmen's and designers' associations. Their members harked back to the teachings of John Ruskin, and strove to extend the practice of William Morris among themselves. As the first, *A. H.Mackmurdo* and *Selwyn Image* formed the *Century Guild* in 1882, which was followed by an *Art Workers' Guild* in 1884. *The Arts and Crafts Exhibition Society* came into being in 1888, with men like *Lewis F. Day, Walter Crane, Heywood Summer*, etc., and related organisations were formed for the spreading of art and the promotion of interest in it in the general public; such organisations included the *Home Arts & Industry Association* of 1885, *The Guild and School of Handicraft*, and *The National Association for the Advancement of Art and its Application to Industry*—both established in 1888. An organisation for Art in the schools followed in the 'nineties. Most of these organisations were formed by men inspired by the principles of Ruskin and Morris, while single designers like Lewis F. Day worked commercially, more upon the principles cherished at the Department of Science and Art. However, none of these contributed anything fundamentally new, as far as theory is concerned, in spite of the great number of books produced by them on every aspect of design. The writings of Lewis F. Day are particularly numerous, and are commendable for their clear exposition of principles. Walter Crane, who became a friend of William Morris and an ardent socialist, subscribed to his political and artistic ideas, and expounded them in books with much vigour, but with far from the same richness of phantasy and human feeling found in the older man. As has already been said, however, it seems true that they contributed little essentially new as far as theory is concerned, and we must therefore be permitted to leave them aside.

It will nevertheless be understood that the teachings of John Ruskin and William Morris had not been seed falling on stony ground. These two had become founders of a school with a highly characteristic outlook, in expressed opposition to the commercial attitude fostered by the Department of Science and Art. The studio craftsman—an individual artist and executor of his own work—belongs to it, and he has played an important part in fashioning our most immediate surroundings ever since. If we turn to the opposite camp, to see what came out of the South Kensington attitude after the days of Sir Henry Cole and Owen Jones, the picture is different, but none the less one of considerable interest.

The influence on the contemporary attitude to design due to the various departmental activities of the 'fifties can only be guessed at, but it must have been considerable. A vast amount of thought and energy was brought to bear on practical and theoretical questions connected with it, and the public was made aware of existing problems and of efforts to solve them. Similarly, the schemes, partly carried out, for extended public education in the art and principles of design, cannot have failed to do a great deal of good, while notable changes can be observed in the design of various products. There was, for example, a strong movement towards flatness in patterns for wallpapers and carpets—and to a somewhat smaller extent in textiles also.[10]

On the whole, it may safely be suggested that a more congenial atmosphere had been created for fresh efforts and out-of-the-way experiments, thus opening the field for single designers working in independence and according to the light of their own experiences. To them, the principles both of Pugin and the pioneer group would be helpful because their general wording on important points rendered them flexible and easily applicable under new conditions, when their application was no longer governed by specific mid-Victorian prejudices. Doubtless even designers and theorists of the Ruskin-Morris school must have been influenced by their work, and have benefited from it in many ways.[11]

As for the establishment at South Kensington, it ceased as early as the middle 'fifties to be a centre of theoretical development, and on the whole it seems as if the theory of design in the last forty years of the century was dominated by the Ruskinian teachings as carried out in practice by Morris.

This must not be taken to mean that the influence from South Kensington counted for nothing, and that the subsequent period saw no theorists who owed allegiance to it. There were at least two very prominent ones; the one, Lewis F. Day, belongs to the last decades of the century, and has already been mentioned in connection with other designers of that time. Although on many points sharing their aspirations, he adopted a commercial attitude to his work; he designed for machine production, and formed his theories of design in direct reference to mechanised industry.

Between the time of Lewis F. Day and the group active in the eighteen-fifties, however, there lived and worked a second designer, whose position was outstanding in the 'sixties and 'seventies. Once counted among the best known designers of his day, he had been completely forgotten by everybody, until his name was brought to light again in the 1930's.[12] He died as recently as 1904; and it was on him, according to Lewis F. Day, that the mantle of Owen Jones seemed at one time to have fallen.[13] His name was *Christopher Dresser;* and he, if anyone, became the heir of the industry-minded pioneers of 1851.

Dresser was born in Glasgow in 1834, the year of William Morris's birth . At thirteen he came to London, and entered the old Schools of Design at Somerset House, where he received training for two years. He then got a scholarship from the school, and began to draw botanical illustrations; later he became lecturer in botany at the Department of Science and Art, and prepared among other matters one of the plates for Owen Jones's *Grammar,* "exhibiting the geometrical arrangement of natural flowers".[14] In 1859 and 1860 he himself published three books on botany.[15]

Apart from articles, Dresser's first writings on design appeared in

1862 with the publication of *The Art of Decorative Design*. This was followed by a series of books and articles, the latter mainly written for the *Furniture Gazette* of which he was the art editor, and in the pages of which numerous examples of his design are to be seen. Among his other books, the most important are *Principles of Decorative Design* (1873), *Studies in Design* (1876), and *Modern Ornamentation* (1886). In 1882 he wrote a book on Japan, whither he had gone in 1876 on an official mission for the British Government; he visited America on his way out, and his travels also included a journey to Vienna in 1873.

Dresser must have set up as a designer at some time in the late 'fifties, and must have become extraordinarily prolific in this trade. At any rate, later in his career he employed several assistants and established first a small studio in Tower Cressy in 1868, then a larger one in 1882 at Wellesley Lodge, Sutton, and later, in 1889, he moved to yet another at Elm Banks, Barnes.[16] His position must have been outstanding, for he was appointed a juror of the World Exhibition at Paris in 1878. Between 1879 and 1882 he acted as art adviser to the Linthorpe Potteries, and also made designs for a number of firms besides being in demand as an interior decorator.[17] According to the *Builder*, he had become well known to English manufacturers at the time of the 1867 Paris Exhibition, and "many of the wall papers, carpets, and textile fabrics shown there bore designs from his pencil";[18] the *Studio* called him "perhaps the greatest of commercial designers", and "a household word to people who are interested in design".[19] Pevsner gives some figures to illustrate the productivity of this man:

in 1869 he sent 158 sketches for silk damasks to Ward's of Halifax, and 67 sketches for carpets to Brinton's, besides many designs for other manufactures; in 1871, 142 carpet designs to Crossley's, etc.[20]

Dresser was also a man of commercial aspirations. At some time in the 'eighties he started an "Art Furniture Alliance," which was an organisation for selling artistically designed furniture, with showrooms in New Bond Street; this was about the time when Morris set up his sales-rooms in Oxford Street. Dresser's establishment was intended "for the sale of metal-work, pottery, glass, fabrics, and other things, the majority being designed by Mr. Dresser himself, or executed under his supervision." The venture was probably meant to exploit the contemporary fashion for "artistic" goods, and it was evidently to this end that "attendants robed in many aesthetic costumes of the period, in demure art colours, added a certain air to the place." However, "so far as memory may be trusted the average work there was very good."[21] Together with a Mr. Holme, Dresser also opened a "new warehouse of Japanese, Chinese, and Indian Art Manufactures" on some sort of wholesale basis, with widespread trade connections in the East.[22] Even if these two enterprises seem to have been failures, they add to our picture of the man: versatile and energetic, artist, writer, and businessman, he established himself in the public eye, where he turned his art to personal and economic account. There is nothing to indicate that Dresser was ever a craftsman in Morris's sense of the word; he seems to have been a commercial designer who never himself worked on the execution of his designs. And where Morris honoured a system of workshop production based on non-mechanical labour, Dresser endeavoured to associate and adapt himself to those very mechanical and commercial forces which Morris shunned, feared, and despised.

Basically, Dresser's principles of design rest on the writings of Owen Jones and others; in his books he paid homage to the *Grammar* and the *Supplementary Report on Design*, and referred to Pugin, Semper, Wornum, and Wyatt. Like Wornum, he held that we "act in accordance with an inward instinct or passion"[23] when we apply colour and ornament to our surrounding objects. He took up the now current recipe for producing ornament—study of natural form and the adaptation of it to ornamental purposes according to principles drawn from a study of ancient art, to "gather from the various styles those broad and general qualities which are applicable in all time and under all circumstances."[24] So, "what I recommend is the production of new forms; but the new compositions may have the vigour of the best Gothic ornament, the severity of Egyptian, the intricacy of the Persian, the gorgeousness of the Alhambra, and so on, only it must not imitate in detail the various styles of the past."[25] We also get general insistence on design to fit material and mode of production, as well as the use for which the object is intended. Floor-patterns should be flat and of a design to be viewed with equal ease from all quarters; designs for wall decorations must not be in conflict with the law of gravity, etc.—in short, design must not offend our sense of reasonableness. Dresser also stressed, as a matter of course, the commercial value of design, and insisted that socially the position of a designer should be on a level with the representational picture-painter, because the importance of his work was no less.

Thus, on all main points he seems to carry on a tradition along those lines which by now were well-established; but only on all *main* points, because in Dresser's whole attitude to design there is a marked and unmistakable shift of emphasis, indicating an increasing interest in design of an abstract nature built on purely artistic values of line, form, and colour—a growing perception of beauty in the functional and non-representational character of these elements. Thus, where for instance the pioneers had said that construction should be ornamented,[26] Dresser held that "a vessel must be constructed, but when formed it need not of necessity be ornamented."[27] This was written in 1873, and in the light of his products at this time and later, I think it supplants his earlier statement, in 1862, when he defined ornament as "that which, superadded to utility, renders the object more acceptable through bestowing upon it an amount of beauty that it would not otherwise possess",[28] and I believe that the different import of these two quotations illustrates the artist's growing predilection for abstraction in design, throwing the emphasis on constructive, instead of ornamental beauty, which he even left out entirely in much of his work. He approved of "carving, sparingly used, . . . and of painted ornament in certain cases", but objected to "whatever is obviously *applied* to the work, and is not a portion of its general fabric." Carving he disliked partly because it collected dust, and he had the unprecedented daring to pronounce curtains superfluous wherever tight-fitting windows would keep out the draught.[29] In short, the putti, dolphins, amorini, the allegorical figures and long-winded inscriptions known from Felix Summerly's products, and even approved by Redgrave in his *Supplementary Report,* are found in Dresser no more. Against the background at least of his own mature work his insistence on appropriateness and fitness of design seems to cover a new meaning, and to carry more weight than ever before.

His predominant interest in formal values was indeed marked even in his first book on *The Art of Decorative Design* (1862), where Chapter V was devoted to "Analysis of Ornamental Forms" on a geometrical basis; patterns were analysed down to their simplest units, and then rearranged in new combinations: "the combination of forms cannot be carried on successfully unless the forms themselves are understood and the conditions of their association ascertained." The next six chapters were then devoted to the study of general principles in the botanical world which might be applied to design; thus, for instance, good botanist that he was, Dresser turned "to the vegetable kingdom in order to discover whether a principle of order prevails throughout the structures which are here presented to us" and found it after a "very cursory glance at the guelder rose," where "the leaves are .... arranged upon the stem in an orderly manner, that they grow in pairs." Subsequent examinations of a similar nature then led to the following conclusion:

as then all plants of a highly organized character, including those which are most esteemed on account of their beauty, are built upon a geometric plan, as the most worthy ornaments have a like basis, and as order most clearly manifests the operation of the mind, we deduce that order is essential to the production of exalted ornament.[30]

Principles of Repetition, of Curves, Proportions, Alternation, and Adaptation were then deduced in a similar manner. Some of these deductions have earlier precedents, the one about curves going back to Owen Jones.

The Art of Decorative Design contains an extraordinary chapter called "The Power of Ornament to express Feelings and Ideas", which strongly echoes the previous interest in symbolism and narrative design. For Dresser was by no means altogether free from this urge towards symbolism, which, however, he turned to personal account: not for him the commonplace and everyday allegorical stuff, such as dreams of mid-Victorian design were usually made of; Dresser's symbolism was fantastic, but significant in the general development of modern design because here again he threw the emphasis on what a modern critic calls the *pure* artistic elements—line, form, and colour, trying to define their psychological suggestive force.

The point of departure in this respect was Dresser's conviction that good ornament possessed a power of expression:

it powerfully affects the spirits. It can soothe as does sweet music, promote mirth as does the merry air, or hush to reverence as does the solemn anthem .... In a thousand strains it speaks, for, like nature 'to the attentive listener it is nowhere dead, never silent.'[31]

This granted, he turns against the current use of hackneyed symbols:

all are agreed as to the desirability of embodying our knowledge in ornamental forms .... but it must be accomplished without the aid of symbols. The appeal must be made to that knowledge which is invariably gained by the common-life experience of those addressed, or to the education which such are known to possess.

Dresser's illustration of his argument was curious. First of all, the artist must undertake "an inquiry into the facts and circumstances which go to make up the mental conception of that which is to be set forth." For example, "what goes to form our conception of evening? Not one fact alone, but a number which we have become familiar with throughout life: it is these which we have to ascertain and discover," in order to play ornamentally with the appropriate mental associations. Among these "facts" are certain aspects of colouring, the

139

brightening "star of the evening"; . . . . The herbage partakes of the influence, and alters the position of its leaves, which for the most part rise and form a more acute angle with the upper portion of the stem. And the majority of flowers close, while others open . . . . The colours are also altered,
etc., etc. Besides these characteristics, there are owls, the moon, mushrooms, bats, "and large-eyed monsters", all of which "contribute to the mental conception of this period of day".

Then, with this our "mental idea of evening" fixed in our mind, "it is not difficult to set forth the thought in ornament, or to create a decorative scheme which shall so impress the mind as to cause it to originate to itself the sense of evening"—and to this end
a few salient features will usually suffice. All that is necessary is that we originate a series of conventional forms which shall call to mind the salient features in our conception, and the result is gained; but the success of the effect will rest upon the character of the ornament, the arrangement of the composition, and the right perception of the characteristic features.

Fig. 21 shows "a hasty sketch in which we have endeavoured to convey the thought of the evening star."[32]

It might be argued that this particular aspect of Dresser's theories does not merit serious attention, because it seems so much like a result of his search for novelty for its own sake, and for the prestige it would give to him; for it seems clear, from the little general knowledge we possess about him, that he was not free from vanity. Now, even if this be so, I do not think it absolves us from considering carefully all aspects of an artist with whom we are seriously concerned; and besides, I do not believe that Dresser's experiments, curious to us, seemed equally curious to his contemporaries; after all, they represent no more than an effort to find new outlets for the interest in symbolism dear to all Victorians; and his products are no more fantastic than those of the Frenchman *Emile Gallé* some decades later, who named one of his cabinets *Forêt Lorraine*, and in intarsia wrote on it: "Tout y parlerait à l'âme en secret Sa douce langue natale. Baudelaire." It should be explained that the cabinet itself is in all respects designed to evoke sentiments like those expressed through its poetical inscription: its legs are carved like peeled sticks, and its plane surfaces are covered with melancholy intarsia landscapes and vegetation.[33]

Compared with Gallé's work, Dresser's manner of treating symbolism is significant because he did *not* carve his furniture into the likeness of peeled sticks, and he did *not* make his meaning obvious through explanatory labels: his manner provides another example of that shift of emphasis alluded to before—it is a shift from a symbolism expressed through representational, more or less imitative forms of ornament, to one which finds its expression through strongly conventionalised forms, where of necessity the more abstract qualities of line, form, and colour must play a predominant part.

Some of the ideas that Dresser sought to express were in themselves abstractions. In one particular sketch used to illustrate this point in his *Principles of Decorative Design* in 1873 *(Fig. 22)*, he wanted

to embody chiefly the one idea of power, energy, force, or vigour; and in order to do this, I have employed such lines as we see in the bursting buds of spring, when the energy of growth is at its maximum, and especially such as are to be seen in the spring growth of a luxuriant tropical vegetation; I have also availed myself of those forms to be seen in certain bones of birds which are associated with the organs of flight, and which give us an impression of great strength, as well as those observable in the powerful propelling fins of certain species of fish.[34]

No doubt can exist that Dresser's preoccupation with the expressive power of ornamental forms acted as a leaven to his work as a designer. There is hardly a single design of his, whether original in form, derived from natural forms, or from one or another of the ancient styles, that does not exhibit this peculiar energy combined with careful planning of parts, and a marked will to definite form, shunning all vagueness. He always carefully considered the effect of his design under various circumstances, as when *(Fig. 23)* he shows "a frieze of new style. This would be used around the upper part of the wall of a room. Being small in detail, it must not be placed high, unless it is enlarged."[35] The frieze exhibits mainly vegetable forms, conventionalised and treated in a two-dimensional manner

141

and interspersed with horizontal and vertical members of some-what uncertain extraction—possibly to some extent derived from vegetable form also. The colours are two shades of green, two each of blue, brown, yellow, and gold, and the forms themselves give some of the same strutting, vigorous feeling as the fish-and-bird-bone design. This is particularly the case with the vertical, column-like members, while some of the flowers in the spaces between them have a softer character altogether.

Dresser's views on furniture and interior furnishings at large, which were based on extensive practice over several years, were set forth in 1873 in his *Principles of Decorative Design*. His broader principles deal exclusively with material and form, saying that

> *the material of which an object is formed should be used in a manner consistent with its own nature, and in that particular way in which it can be most easily 'worked'.... when an object is about to be formed, that material (or those materials) which is (or are) most appropriate to its formation should be sought and employed.*

Other principles echo Jones in the *Grammar*, as when Dresser insisted that *"curves will be found to be beautiful just as they are subtle in character; those which are most subtle in character being most beautiful;"* and about proportions, that *"proportion, like the curve, must be of a subtle nature."* Other rules based on the study of the vegetable world in *The Art of Decorative Design* say that *"a principle of order must prevail in every ornamental composition ... The orderly repetition of parts frequently aids in the production of ornamental effects ... Alternation is a principle of primary importance in certain ornamental compositions,"* and a rule on conventionalisation: *"If plants are employed as ornaments they must not be treated imitatively, but must be conventionally treated, or rendered into ornament."* It will be seen that all these rules deal with the material and formal elements of design in the most general way; for Dresser did not "attempt to express what character forms should have in order that they be considered beautiful," but contented himself "by saying that they must be truthful in expression, and graceful, delicate, and refined in contour, manifesting no coarseness .... the beautiful is loveable."[36] Similarly, to his remarks on colour, largely built on Owen Jones and Field, he added his own very sensible observation that "there are, however, subtleties of harmony which it is difficult to understand." The *arbiter elegantiarum* in these respects would be found in "the opinions of men who have cultivated their sense and perception of the beautiful throughout a long series of years," as well as in "those practices which have received the sanction of the masters of the great art-epochs, and [which] commend themselves to our judgement by fitness and consistency." Reason, experience, and feeling should jointly be brought to bear on any judgement of design, and the day was gone when cut-and-dried principle reigned supreme.

Laying down rules for the design of furniture, Dresser was again concerned about material and form. Following Jones, the general form should be first considered "and every effort should be made at securing to the general mass beauty of shape". This done, there follows the division "into primary and secondary parts .... with reference to the laws of proportion", and then

detail and enrichment may now be considered; but while these cannot be too excellent, they must still be subordinate in obtrusiveness to the general mass, or to the aspect of the work as a whole.

Finally, he stressed the importance of finding "the most convenient or appropriate form for an object .... the consideration of utility must in all cases precede the consideration of beauty."[37] This statement was followed by an analysis of structural strength and other qualities of wood, illustrating and criticising examples of furniture from the works of Charles Eastlake and Bruce Talbert. Unlike Owen Jones, Dresser disapproved of all false imitations, such as the graining of wood or imitations in one material of a technique proper to another. He was also afraid of a too high degree of "excessive finish", which he found "often (but by no means always) destroys art-effect"; also he rejected all manner of "pretence in art and art-decoration" in strong terms.[38]

The examples he gives of his own design are few in number, comprising a sofa and some chairs only, of a sturdy construction, ornamented with very discreet carving—abstract design in flat relief—and with inlaid or painted ornament of an abstract or formalised vegetable kind. Padding is reduced to what is necessary for reasonable comfort, and all the constructive members are clearly shown in obvious relation to the entire structural design. A piece of furniture like the chair in *Fig. 24* may or may not appeal to contemporary taste; but it conforms in its constructive features to Dresser's own principles, and exhibits a sober and restrained scheme of decoration clearly planned to underline the general form and show it to advantage.

However, Dresser's most remarkable achievements were in the fields of pottery, glass, and silver work. In these ductile and pliable materials he could experiment freely in his search for a form which combined aesthetic and functional qualities, and the result was a series of objects some of which have been illustrated in his own *Principles of Decorative Design*, some in Nikolaus Pevsner's article on Dresser in the *Architectural Review*, some in the *Studio*, and some in the Victoria and Albert Museum exhibition of *Victorian and Edwardian Design* in 1952–53.

The general design of these objects was determined by some theoretical considerations, set down in the *Principles of Decorative Design*, concerning the artistic treatment of material and special techniques of production and workmanship; there is the well-known insistence on flat decoration, the character of which should be determined by the nature of the object which it adorns. Simplicity and good sense should be ruling principles—"no plate should have a landscape painted upon it, nor a figure, nor a group of flowers," because in such an object of necessity, destined to be viewed from all sides, "whatever has a right and wrong way upwards is inappropriate."[39] Dresser's ceramic works, dating from the late 'seventies and onwards, show inspiration largely from pre-Columbian Latin-American forms, and rely for effect solely on outline, form, and the artistic exploitation of glaze; in this particular respect he received valuable assistance from Henry Tooth, who worked with him and ran the factory at Linthorpe from 1879 onwards.[40]

In his designs for glass, Dresser seems to have been influenced by Arabic and Persian as well as Roman forms. The examples of his work illustrated here *(Fig. 25)*, speak for his understanding of the particular facilities offered by this material, and his freedom from contemporary conventions in availing himself of them. The objects probably date from between 1880 and 1890, and like other well-known pieces, they were evidently executed by James Cooper & Son, Glasgow, producers of *Clutha* glass. Earlier glass designs, illustrated in *Principles of Decorative Design*, show more restrained forms and indicate a development towards greater freedom in the later works.

When we regard an object like the electroplate teapot at *Fig. 26*, however, we have before us a type which has its roots at least as far back as 1873, when several designs of a similar nature were illustrated in *Principles of Decorative Design*. This teapot is of a later date (ca. 1880),[41] but it has been chosen as one of the extremely few objects of its kind which have been traced, and because it embodies almost to perfection principles which its author had developed at least seven years earlier. For that date, to which in type the teapot belongs, it is a truly amazing work.

Amazing first and foremost because it is a representative and expensive *objet d'art*, altogether of such a nature as to be taken for a work with aesthetic pretensions; and yet we find these pretensions satisfied by nothing but strict adherence to functional form, and the aesthetic exploitation of beautiful material. The pot is designed so as to stand firmly on the table, with a central hole evidently for a heating spirit flame. The lid is simply arranged to admit of easy filling, and the handle and spout are designed so as to allow easy pouring without undue exercise of the wrist; in *Studies of Decorative Design* a lengthy passage was devoted to making this important consideration a matter of rule, and a similar consideration, it will be recalled, determined the shape of Henry Cole's milk jug in 1847. The only fault in this design, from a practical point of view, is that the lid is fixed in front, so that the liquid seems likely to overflow before running out of the spout if the pot should be very full of tea. This was a fault against which Dresser had given special warning.[42] While meeting all these practical demands, it is easily seen how the designer has turned utilitarian features to decorative account: the spout is so proportioned as to fit the corpus harmoniously, being of a square section to conform to the right angle between its vertical and horizontal planes. The mouth of the spout, having been given a form to minimise dripping, is also terminated upwards on lines which give added character to the design. The metal bars of the handle meet the surface of the corpus with considerable elegance, and the wooden part of it—black ebony to contrast with the shining surface of silvery metal—has a twisted upper termination, an extra accent, a small softening detail in a somewhat firm design. Altogether, this practical little "instrument", one might almost say, contains features of beauty which may well surprise, considering that as a type it takes us right back into the 'seventies. In time we shall probably have to go all the way back to Queen Anne to find a design of similar character, where simplicity of body and line have been exploited to the utmost; or, towards our own time, we reach the late 'twenties and early 'thirties before we again see objects of a similar frank honesty and a like self-sufficiency of artistic means. If he only had this single object to his credit, it is not too much to say that Dresser broke through the barrier between the Victorians and ourselves, and led the practice of design, as well as its theory, up to the threshold of our own time.

Sad to say, from our point of view the later part of Dresser's career does not fulfil the promise of his youth. He seems to have exploited the changing fashions of the day, and to a great extent abstained from striking out further new roads for himself. The last twenty years or so of his life, therefore, deserve no comment in the present context.

SOME COMMENTS
AND A LEGACY

On working my way through the mass of printed matter which has given substance to the preceding pages, there have also passed through my mind reflections of a kind not sufficiently relevant in the present context to warrant inclusion in this book. I have also been delighted at the wealth of material to be found, at the surprising number of people caring about design in a period which has been generally considered to mark the lowest point in the history of the art, at the many surprising theoretical tendencies, and, not least, at the great richness and variety of the work of English designers throughout almost two-thirds of a century.

My work has been particularly rewarding to me because so many previously unknown persons have come within my vision: others, only dimly seen or understood before, have, as it seems, revealed their personalities in all their complexity, as in the case of Ruskin and Morris. And through all these, as well as by other ways and means, fascinating aspects of the Victorian mind, and of England itself at that time, have been disclosed.

Some notions have also presented themselves in the course of my work, which are even closer to the heart of the matter. We have, for instance, seen how several trends of thought asserted themselves and became influential in English Victorian design; how the Catholic Gothicism of Pugin existed side by side with the commercial attitude of the Henry Cole group, and how they were

147

both scorned by the Protestant-ethical attitude of John Ruskin; and yet I feel that they may all be united under the common denominator of a symbolistic or narrative attitude to design. This is true also of prominent younger contemporaries; it is true of William Morris, when he insists on some kind of "mystery" to be embodied in his craft, and strives to make it speak of the things of "the lovely earth". It is true of Christopher Dresser when he produces his fish-and-bird-bone compositions, expressive of the power inherent in vegetable and animal form. More than any other I should therefore hold this trait to be typical of Victorian design—most strongly expressed in its earlier phase, less pronounced later on, when room was allowed beside it for an aesthetic of forms mainly depending on line, colour, and shape.

To this part of the period, therefore, should be directed the attention of anyone mainly interested in tracing the origin of modern functionalism in the minor arts as far as the 19th century is concerned. Functionalism, as we know it especially from the 1930's, implies that an object should be pre-eminently useful and practical; it implies the axiom that what is practical is also beautiful; and it excludes from the language of aesthetics the various kinds of associative ornament. It will be understood that neither Pugin, Ruskin, nor the associates of Henry Cole, have anything to do with an attitude like this; and only with great reservations may the name of William Morris be cited as a propagator of an eminently rational turn of mind.

In the case of Christopher Dresser, however, we see an artist who in some of his work adopts a clear functionalistic attitude. The same is true of William Godwin's "Japanese" furniture, and of a great number of pieces produced by still later people like Mackmurdo, Annesley Voysey, C. R. Ashbee, and others—not to mention the houses built by the Scottish architect C. R. Mackintosh. They carry on the tradition from Whistler's White House built for him in Chelsea in 1877 by E. W. Godwin.

The position of William Morris as an artist and as a source of inspiration remains of course unchallenged, despite the attention which should also be given to some of his contemporaries. Between them they all produced a wide range of high-class works with a wide variety of expression, untrammelled by the somewhat rigid awkwardness that often characterises the efforts of the earlier men who had tried to establish a new order; and with all these, British design at long last seemed on the way to recapture its leading position in Europe, which had been lost a century earlier with the progress of the Napoleonic wars. Now British work was being represented and admired at major exhibitions all over Europe and in America; the greatest foreign art-periodicals wrote of it with respect, and Britons were called on important artistic missions abroad; to the propagators of the once so promising movements of *Jugend* and *Art Nouveau,* the names of Ruskin and Morris were intimately known, and their books were read by them with reverence.

I wrote in my introduction that Victorian theories of design point to the conflict which was bound to arise when the established tradition of craftsmanship and workshop manufacture in the crafts was in a comparatively short time broken, and replaced by mechanical mass production on a predominantly commercial basis; and that the growth of a Victorian theory of design is therefore the story of adjustment to a new and somewhat perplexing state of affairs.

However, after more than fifty years of struggle and of thought, a solution *was* found on British soil. At the end of the Victorian era, and in the subsequent first decade of King Edward's reign, while the entire new movement was still flourishing, attempts were also made at uniting the two opposing camps of theorists: on the one hand, in the manner of William Dyce, and Henry Cole, and Owen Jones, and Christopher Dresser, to acknowledge modern mechanised industry not as an evil necessity, but as a basic element of production. And, while doing this, to subject it on the other hand as far as possible to artistic will, and to use it not by way of commercial enterprise for the production of low-quality or ugly wares, but to shape on beautiful lines objects for common and everyday use. C. R. Ashbee, with his Guild of Handicraft and his School of Arts and Crafts, is the chief progenitor of this school of thought—an artist and an organizer of outstanding ability. Through his education as an architect and through the leanings of his whole personality he felt kinship with the beliefs of Ruskin and Morris, and responded to their humanism. This became an integral part of his own programme; but with the greater understanding of a younger man he ventured to combine it with the forces of modern industry. His writings and his activities merit a profounder study than can be given them here, however intimately connected with Victorian theories of design they may be. His works seem to me to point ahead and lead on to a far more international field of study, where an answer must also be sought to the entire question of existing connections between British design and that of France, Belgium, Scandinavia, and the German-speaking countries. Attention would also have to be given to the subsequent history of the new movement in England and Scotland, and to the sad story of its decline during the years before the first World War. Here lies rich material for research, and it is to be hoped that it will be undertaken before long.

To the artist and the industrialist of today the legacy of this movement—the experience of half a century or more of practical and theoretical work—should constitute an admonition to ceaseless effort and firm belief in the possibility of investing even the mechanical product of modern industry with some of the mental richness of the past.

APPENDIX I

A. N. W. PUGIN

Letter to Adolphe-Napoléon Didron.

From B. Ferrey, *Recollections of A. N. Welby Pugin,* London, 1861,
pp. 235—239.

"Monsieur,

"Je suis fort content d'apprendre que le désir de restaurer le véritable art chrétien, si longtemps négligé, se représent avec force en France. On doit encourager de pareilles tentatives, et je vous donnerai sur mes travaux, avec le plus grand plaisir, tous les renseignemens qui pourraient vous être utiles. Mes travaux ne se bornent pas aux monumens religieux; je m'attache encore à la restauration des moindres accessoires, et je m'occupe même des étoffes pour les chapes et les chasubles. Je n'ai pas besoin de vous dire en effet que rien n'est plus choquant à l'esprit d'un véritable connaisseur de l'art chrétien que de voir une église magnifique avec des autels, des chandeliers et des ornemens dans le style moderne ou *rococo,* comme ceux qu'on trouve dans les plus belles cathédrales de la France et de la Belgique. J'ai donc établi, il y a quatre ans à peu près, des fabriques de tous les objets qui peuvent contribuer à la décoration et à la richesse des monumens ecclésiastiques.

"Dans ces fabriques, on confectionne des objets en or, en argent et en cuivre, tels que burettes, calices, ciboires, ostensoirs, chandeliers, lampes, couronnes ardentes, tabernacles en forme de tour, croix processionales, reliquaires, châsses, et enfin tous ce qui appartient au culte catholique. J'ai fait copier ces objets d'après modèles anciens avec la plus grande exactitude, et je suis parvenu à former des ouvriers qui travaillent tout-à-fait dans l'ancien style. Les calices, larges à la coupe, sont posés sur des pieds émaillés, même enrichis de pierreries et dessinés dans des formes géométriques. Les chandeliers sont de toute grandeur, mais moins élevés que ceux qui s'exécutent à présent. Je n'ai pas trouvé dans les autorités anciennes que les chandeliers fussent très-élevés autrefois. Je dois vous dire que ces objets sont exécutés dans l'ancienne manière. Ils sont ciselés, gravés, émaillés, battus, et non pas coulés en fonte comme à l'habitude de faire aujourd'hui. Le procédé de la fonte rend tous ces ouvrages lourds, tandis que les anciens ornemens en métal sont legers et travaillés avec art et sentiment. Pour les ostensoirs et les reliquaires, j'ai imité les plus beaux qu'on trouve en Belgique.

"J'ai fait faire pour les cierges une couronne ardente qui a trente-six pieds de circonférence. Elle est chargée en écussons couverts d'inscriptions et suspendue avec des chaînes ornées. Lorsqu'elle est allumée pour les grandes fêtes, cela produit un effet magnifique.

"J'espère que le temps n'est pas éloigné où tous les mauvais lustres, qui préviennent des salles de bal et qu'on voit aujourd'hui dans les églises, seront remplacés par des couronnes de cuivre doré qui sont d'un caractère tout-à-fait ecclésiastique. J'ai déjà envoyé en Amérique plusieurs ornemens de ce genre, et toutes les églises que j'ai bâties sont décorées d'objets qui portent le même caractère et sont dans le style de l'époque reproduite par le monument. L'autel de la chapelle de la Sainte Vierge, dans l'église de Birmingham, est extrêmement riche, et dans le style Gothique du temps de Saint Louis. Il porte un tabernacle précieux en forme de tour, orné de pierreries et des quatre évangélistes en émail. Cet autel est tout couvert de bas-reliefs dorés et peints dans le style chrétien; de chaque côté sont suspendus des rideaux richement brodés. Tous nos autels ont des rideaux, comme on en voit dans les tableaux anciens et dans les miniatures. Nous avons plusieurs triptyques avec des portes couvertes de peintures; nous les plaçons au-dessus des autels dans les chapelles. J'ai parfaitement réussi à faire des pavés incrustés; l'église de Nottingham sera pavée de ces briques émaillées de différentes couleurs, chargées d'inscriptions et de divers ornemens colorés en bleu, rouge, jaune et vert. Ces pavés produisent un effet magnifique, et rappellent la richesse des vitraux peints. Les vitraux de couleur, si essentiels aux églises, sont bien faits chez nous. Un morceau de verre épais, attaché par le plomb, ne porte qu'un seule couleur. Je ne cherche pas à faire des tableaux sur verre, mais à suivre la sévérités des anciens verriers qui accordaient leur style avec l'architecture des fenêtres. Vous seriez forte content, j'en suis bien sûr, des vitraux que j'ai placés dans les églises que j'ai fait construire. Tout ce que je cherche c'est de restaurer ce qu'on faisait anciennement, et non pas d'inventer de nouveaux procédés qui ne réussissent jamais. Quant aux draps d'or et de soie, quant aux galons, je les ai copiés sur des tombeaux anciens d'évêques et d'autres ecclésiastiques, et j'en ai fait faire une assez grande quantité. J'aurai très-grand plaisir de vous envoyer des échantillons de ces galons qui sont fort légers. Avec cette lettre, je vous adresse la gravure de quelques-unes des briques incrustées dont je surveille l'exécution. La liste suivante des travaux que je dirige pourra vous être utils."

[Here he gives a list of his finest churches, etc.]

"Je compte commencer quatre églises nouvelles dans le courant de l'année 1843.

"Tous ces bâtimens sont construits dans le véritable style chrétien. Ils sont plus ou moins riches dans les détails; plusieurs ont des murailles et des plafonds chargés de peintures et de dorures. Les autels, les fonts baptismaux, et surtout les jubés qui séparent les chœurs et qui portent le grand crucifix, les images de la Sainte Vierge et de Saint Jean, sont tous dans le même style. J'espère que vous viendrez un jour ici pour voir ce que nous avons fait. L'église de Saint Georges à Londres vous fera plaisir; elle a 246 pieds de long.* Le clocher aura 317 pieds de hauteur jusqu'à la croix de la flèche. Je vous adresse un paquet de gravures pour vous donner une idée de ces constructions.

"J'aurais grand plaisir à vous envoyer des renseignemens plus précis sur tout ce que vous voulez savoir, et je reste, Monsieur, votre serviteur bien dévoué,   *"A. Welby Pugin."*

* "The base of this tower is only yet built, and according to present appearances there seems little hope of the structure being ever completed according to Pugin's design." (Ferrey's note. The French spelling of Pugin's letter, not entirely correct, is reproduced from Ferrey's book.)

APPENDIX II

"General Principles in the Arrangement
of Form and Colour, in Architecture and
the Decorative Arts, which are advocated
throughout this Work."

From Owen Jones,

T h e   G r a m m a r   o f   O r n a m e n t,

London, 1868,

1st ed., London, 1856.

Proposition 1.

The Decorative Arts arise from, and should properly be attendant upon, Architecture.

Proposition 2.

Architecture is the material expression of the wants, the faculties, and the sentiments, of the age in which it is created.

Style in Architecture is the peculiar form that expression takes under the influence of climate and materials at command.

Proposition 3.

As Architecture, so all works of the Decorative Arts, should possess fitness, proportion, harmony, the result of all which is repose.

Proposition 4.

True beauty results from that repose which the mind feels when the eye, the intellect, and the affections, are satisfied from the absence of any want.

Proposition 5.

Construction should be decorated. Decoration should never be purposely constructed.

That which is beautiful is true;
that which is true must be beautiful.

Proposition 6.

Beauty of form is produced by lines growing out one from the other in gradual undulations: there are no excrescences; nothing could be removed and leave the design equally good or better.

Proposition 7.

The general forms being first cared for, these should be subdivided and ornamented by general lines; the interstices may then be filled in with ornament, which may again be subdivided and enriched for closer inspection.

Proposition 8.

All ornament should be based upon a geometrical construction.

Proposition 9.

As in every perfect work of Architecture a true proportion will be found to reign between all the members which compose it, so throughout the Decorative Arts every assemblage of forms should be arranged on certain definite proportions; the whole and each particular member should be a multiple of some simple unit.

Those proportions will be the most beautiful which it will be most difficult for the eye to detect.

Thus the proportion of a double square, or 4 to 8, will be lesss beautiful than the more subtle ratio of 5 to 8; 3 to 6, than 3 to 7; 3 to 9, than 3 to 8; 3 to 4, than 3 to 5.

Proposition 10.

Harmony of form consists in the proper balancing, and contrast of, the straight, the inclined, and the curved.

Proposition 11.

In surface decoration all lines should flow out of a parent stem. Every ornament, however distant, should be traced to its branch and root. *Oriental practice.*

Proposition 12.

All junctions of curved lines with curved or of curved lines with straight should be tangential to each other. *Natural law. Oriental practice in accordance with it.*

Proposition 13.

Flowers or other natural objects should not be used as ornaments, but conventional representations founded upon them sufficiently suggestive to convey the intended image to the mind, without destroying the unity of the object they are employed to decorate. *Universally obeyed in the best periods of Art, equally violated when Art declines.*

Proposition 14.

Colour is used to assist in the development of form, and to distinguish objects or parts of objects one from another.

Proposition 15.

Colour is used to assist light and shade, helping the undulations of form by the proper distribution of the several colours.

Proposition 16.

These objects are best attained by the use of the primary colours on small surfaces and in small quantities, balanced and supported by the secondary and tertiary colours on the larger masses.

Proposition 17.

The primary colours should be used on the upper portions of objects, the secondary and tertiary on the lower.

Proposition 18.

(Field's Chromatic equivalents.)

The primaries of equal intensities will harmonise or neutralise each other, in the proportions of 3 yellow, 5 red, and 8 blue, — integrally as 16.

The secondaries in the proportions of 8 orange, 13 purple, 11 green, — integrally as 32.

The tertiaries, citrine (compound of orange and green), 19; russet (orange and purple), 21; olive (green and purple), 24; — integrally as 64.

It follows that, —

Each secondary being a compound of two primaries is neutralised by the remaining primary in the same proportions: thus, 8 of orange by 8 of blue, 11 of green by 5 of red, 13 of purple by 3 of yellow.

Each tertiary being a binary compound of two secondaries, is neutralised by the remaining secondary: as, 24 of olive by 8 of orange, 21 of russet by 11 of green, 19 of citrine by 13 of purple.

Proposition 19.

The above supposes the colours to be used in their prismatic intensities, but each colour has a varity of *tones* when mixed with white, or of *shades* when mixed with gray or black.

When a full colour is contrasted with another of a lower tone, the volume of the latter must be proportionally increased.

Proposition 20.

Each colour has a variety of *hues,* obtained by admixture with other colours, in addition to white, grey, or black: thus we have of yellow, — orange-yellow on the one side, and lemon-yellow on the other; so of red, — scarlet-red, and crimson-red; and of each every variety of *tone* and *shade.*

When a primary tinged with another primary is contrasted with a secondary, the secondary must have a hue of the third primary.

Proposition 21.

In using the primary colours on moulded surfaces, we should place blue, which retires, on the concave surfaces; yellow, which advances, on the convex; and red, the intermediate colour, on the undersides; separating the colours by white on the vertical planes.

When the proportions required by Proposition 18 cannot be obtained, we may procure the balance by a change in the colours themselves: thus, if the surfaces to be coloured should give too much yellow, we should make the red more crimson and the blue more purple, — *i. e.* we should take the yellow out of them; so if the surfaces should give too much blue, we should make the yellow more orange and the red more scarlet.

Proposition 22.

The various colours should be so blended that the objects coloured, when viewed at a distance, should present a neutralised bloom.

Proposition 23.

No composition can ever be perfect in which any one of the three primary colours is wanting, either in its natural state or in combination.

Proposition 24.

When two tones of the same colour are juxtaposed, the light colour will appear lighter, and the dark colour darker.

Proposition 25.

When two different colours are juxtaposed, they receive a double modification; first, as to their tone (the light colour appearing lighter, and the dark colour appearing darker); secondly, as to their hue, each will become tinged with the complementary colour of the other.

Proposition 26.

Colours on white grounds appear darker; on black grounds, lighter.

Proposition 27.

Black grounds suffer when opposed to colours which give a luminous complementary.

Proposition 28.

Colours should never be allowed to impinge upon each other.

Proposition 29.

When ornaments in a colour are on a ground of a contrasting colour, the ornament should be separated from the ground by an edging of lighter colour; as a red flower on a green ground should have an edging of lighter red.

Proposition 30.

When ornaments in a colour are on a gold ground, the ornaments should be separated from the ground by an edging of a darker colour.

Proposition 31.

Gold ornaments on any coloured ground should be outlined with black.

Proposition 32.

Ornaments of any colour may be separated from grounds of any other colour by edgings of white, gold, or black.

Proposition 33.

Ornaments in any colour, or in gold, may be used on white or black grounds, without outline or edging.

Proposition 34.

In "self-tints," tones, or shades of the same colour, a light tint on a dark ground may be used without outline; but a dark ornament on a light ground requires to be outlined with a still darker tint.

Proposition 35.

Imitations, such as the graining of woods, and of the various coloured marbles, allowable only, when the employment of the thing imitated would not have been inconsistent.

Proposition 36.

The principles discoverable in the works of the past belong to us; not so the results. It is taking the end for the means.

Proposition 37.

No improvement can take place in the Art of the present generation until all classes, Artists, Manufacturers, and the Public, are better educated in Art, and the existence of general principles is more fully recognised.

BIBLIOGRAPHY

Manuscript Material

A. H. MACKMURDO, *History of the Arts and Crafts Movement*. Typescript, with corrections in M.'s hand. Preface written in M.'s hand. The work is divided into nine chapters, each paginated from p. 1; chs. II and III paginated continuously. The whole 258 pp. No date.

Mackmurdo's *unpublished monograph*. Typescript, corrected in M.'s own hand. Three last pages also in M.'s hand. 20 pp. No date, but probably *c.* 1936, because of affixed postcard stamped 7 Feb. 1936, giving information for the monograph.

Both papers are in the possession of Mrs. McQueen, and were lent to the Victoria and Albert Museum in the winter of 1952–53.

BIBLIOGRAPHY

Periodicals

The Architectural Review, 1896—
The Art Journal, 1839—1912.
The Art Workers' Quarterly, 1902—06.
The Athenaeum, 1828—1921.
The Builder, 1842—
The Cabinet-maker, 1880—1936.
The Cornhill Magazine, 1860—
The Furniture Gazette, 1873—93.
The Illustrated London News, 1842—
The Journal of Design and Manufacture, 1849—52.
The Journal of the Royal Institute of British Architects, 1893—
Reports from Committees.
Statutes at Large.
The Studio, 1893—
The Times, 1788—

Books and Articles

ALBERT, *The Principal Speeches and Addresses of H. R. H. the Prince Consort*, Lond. 1862.
THE ART JOURNAL, *Exhibition Volume*, Lond. 1851.
ARTS AND CRAFTS EXHIBITION SOCIETY, *Arts and Crafts Essays*, by Members of the Arts and Crafts Exhibition Society, Lond. 1893.
Catalogue of the Exhibitions 1888—1903.
B., 'On the Government Schools of Design', *The Art Journal*, Sept. and Dec. 1849, XI 270—271, 372—374.
BURNE-JONES, LADY G., *Memorials of Edward Burne-Jones*, I—II, Lond. 1904.
BURY, T., 'Obituary Note on A. W. N. Pugin', *The Builder*, Sept. 1852, X 605—07.
CLAPHAM, J. H., *An Economic History of Modern Britain. The Early Railway Age 1820—1850*, Cambr. 1950.
CLARK, SIR KENNETH, *The Gothic Revival*, 2nd ed. Lond. 1950.
COLE, SIR HENRY, 'Decoration', *The Athenaeum*, 30 Dec. 1843, 1074—75, 1114—15, 1162—64.
Art-manufactures, collected by Felix Summerly, 6th ed. Chiswick 1847.
Fifty Years of Public Work, I—II, Lond. 1884.
COLE, H., and REDGRAVE, R., *Addresses of the Superintendents of the Department of Practical Art*, Lond. 1853.
COLLINGWOOD, W. G., *The Art Teaching of John Ruskin*, Lond. 1891.

159

CORNELL, E., *De stora utställningarnas arkitekturhistoria*, Stockholm 1952.

CRANE, W., *An Artist's Reminiscences*, Lond. and N. Y. 1907.

William Morris to Whistler: Papers and Addresses on Art and Craft and the Commonweal, Lond. 1911.

CRANE, W., and DAY, L. F., *Moot Points — Friendly Disputes on Art and Industry*, Lond. 1903.

DAY, L. F., 'Victorian Progress in Applied Design', *The Art Journal Royal Jubilee Number*, June 1887, new series VII, 185—202.

'William Morris and his Art', *The Art Journal Easter Art Annual*, 1899.

DICKENS, C., *Hard Times*, The London Edition, The Caxton Publishing Co. First publ. 1854.

DRESSER, C., *Development of Ornamental Art in the International Exhibition*, Lond. 1862.

The Art of Decorative Design, Lond. 1862.

'Principles in Design', nine articles, *The Technical Educator*, 1870, I.

Principles of Decorative Design, 3rd ed. Lond., Paris and N. Y. 1873 (this is the date given to entry in Bodleian Library Catalogue).

Studies in Design, Lond., Paris and N. Y. 1876 (this is the date given to entry in Bodleian Library Catalogue).

'Art Industries', 'Art Museums', 'Art Schools', 3 lectures delivered in Philadelphia, *Penn Monthly*, Jan., Feb., March 1877.

Modern Ornamentation, Lond. 1886.

DYCE, W., *Introduction to the Drawingbook of the School of Design*, Lond. 1842—3. Publ. by the Dept. of Science and Art, Chapman and Hall, Lond. 1854. Printed in J. D., 1851, VI 1—6.

EASTLAKE, C. L., 'The Fashion of Furniture', *The Cornhill Magazine*, March 1864, IX 337—349.

Hints on Household Taste, Lond. 1868.

A History of the Gothic Revival, Lond. 1872.

FERREY, B., *Recollections of A. N. Welby Pugin, and his Father, Augustus Pugin; with Notices of their Works*, Lond. 1861.

FFRENCHE, Y., *The Great Exhibition 1851*, Lond .1950.

FIELD, G., *Chromatography: or, a Treatise on Colours and Pigments, and of their Power in Painting*, etc., Lond. 1835.

FIELDING, K. J., 'Charles Dickens and the Department of Practical Art', *Modern Language Review*, July 1953 XLVIII 270–277.

FLOUD, PETER, 'William Morris as an Artist: A New View', *The Listener*, October 7th and 14th 1954.

GAUNT, W., *The Aesthetic Adventure*, Oxf. 1945.

GIBBS-SMITH, C. H., *The Great Exhibition of 1851, A Commemorative Album*, Lond. 1950.

GIEDION, S., *Space, Time, and Architecture: The Growth of a New Tradition*, 8th enlarged ed., Oxf. 1949.
Mechanization Takes Command. A Contribution to Anonymous History. Oxf. and N. Y. 1948.

GODWIN, E. W., *Dress and its Relation to Health and Climate*, Lond. 1884.

THE GREAT EXHIBITION, *Official Descriptive and Illustrated Catalogue*, I–III, Lond. 1851.

GRENNAN, M. R., *William Morris, Medievalist and Revolutionary*, N. Y. 1945.

GREY, L. E., *William Morris; Prophet of England's New Order*, Lond., Toronto, Melbourne, Sydney and Wellington 1949.

HARBRON, D., *The Conscious Stone; the Life of Edward William Godwin*, Lond. 1949.

HAY, D. R., *The Laws of Harmonious Colouring, Adapted to Interior Decorations, etc., to which is added An Attempt to Define Aesthetic Taste*, 5th ed., Lond. and Edinburgh 1844. First publ. 1828.
Original Geometrical Diaper Designs, accompanied by An Attempt to Develope and Elucidate the True Principles of Ornamental Design, as Applied to the Decorative Arts, Lond. and Edinburgh 1844.

HENDERSON, PHIL., *The Letters of William Morris*, Lond., N. Y. and Toronto 1950.

HITCHCOCK, HENRY-RUSSEL, *Early Victorian Architecture in Britain*, Yale 1954 I–II.

HOBHOUSE, C., *1851 and the Crystal Palace*, Lond. 1950.

HOPE, H. R., *The Sources of Art Nouveau*, unpubl. doctoral thesis, the Division of Fine Arts, Harvard University, Dec. 1942.

HORNE, H. P., 'The Century Guild', *The Art Journal*, Sept. 1887, N. S. VII, 295–298.

HUEFFER, F. M., 'A Note on the Work of Ford Madox Brown', *Catalogue to the Fifth Exhibition of the Arts and Crafts Exhibition Society*, 1896, 11–28.
The Pre-Raphaelite Brotherhood, Lond. and N. Y., no date, but obviously after 1905.

JONES, OWEN, *The Grammar of Ornament*, Lond. 1856. For present work, ed. of 1868.
The True and the False in the Decorative Arts, Lond. 1863. Built on lectures delivered June 1852 at Marlborough House.

KERR, R., 'On the Life of Welby Pugin', *The Builder*, May 1862, XX 345–346, 364–367.

KONODY, P. G., *The Art of Walter Crane*, Lond. 1902.

161

KUNSTGEWERBEMUSEUM ZÜRICH, *Um 1900. Art Nouveau und Jugendstil.*Wegleitung 194 des Kunstgewerbemuseums Zürich. Zürich 1952.

LADD, H., *The Victorian Morality in Art. An Analysis of Ruskin's Ethics.* N. Y. 1932.

LAZARUS, EMMA, 'A Day in Surrey with William Morris', *The Century Magazine*, July 1886, XXXII 388—397.

LENNING, H. F., *The Art Nouveau*, The Hague 1951.

LEON, D., *Ruskin, the Great Victorian*, Lond. 1949.

LOWRY, J., *The Japanese Influence on Victorian Design*, unpublished lecture given at the Victoria and Albert Museum, London, Dec. 1952.

MACKAIL, J. W., *The Life of William Morris*, I—II, Lond. 1899. For this work, ed. Oxford University Press, The World's Classics, 1950.
Introduction to Catalogue of an Exhibition of the Work of William Morris at the Municipal School of Art, Manchester, Oct. 1908.

MADSEN, STEPHAN TSCHUDI, 'Viktoriansk Dekorativ Kunst', *Nordenfjeldske Kunstindustrimuseums Årbok*, Trondheim 1952, 9—92.
Sources of Art Nouveau, Oslo, 1956.

MARILLIER, H. C., *History of the Merton Abbey Tapestry Works*, Lond. 1927.

MORRIS, MAY, *William Morris, Artist, Writer, Socialist*, I—II, Oxf. 1936.

MORRIS, WILLIAM, *The Collected Works of William Morris*, I—XXIV, Lond. 1910—15.
The Nature of Gothic: a Chapter from the Stones of Venice by John Ruskin, with a Preface by William Morris, Orpington and Lond. 1899.

THE NATIONAL ASSOCIATION FOR THE ADVANCEMENT OF ART AND ITS APPLICATION TO INDUSTRY, *Transactions*, Lond. 1888—90.

PEVSNER, N., 'William Morris, C. R. Ashbee und das zwanzigste Jahrhundert', *Deutsche Vierteljahrsschrift für Literaturwissenschaft und Geistesgeschichte*, Halle, XIV, Heft iv, 536—562.
Pioneers of the Modern Movement from William Morris to Walter Gropius, Lond. 1936.
'Christopher Dresser, Industrial Designer', *The Architectural Review*, Apr. 1937, LXXXI 183—186.
Academies of Art, Past and Present, Cambr. 1940.
'A Short Pugin Florilegium', *Architectural Review*, Aug.1943, XCIV 31—34.
Matthew Digby Wyatt, Cambr. 1950.
High Victorian Design, Lond. 1951.

PIPER, J., 'St. Marie's Grange, The First Home of A. W. N. Pugin', *The Architectural Review*, Oct. 1945, XCVIII 90—93.

PUGIN, A., and PUGIN, A. N. W., literary part by E. J. Willson, *Examples of Gothic Architecture, I—II*, Lond. 1831—36.

PUGIN, A. N. W., *Contrasts*, Lond. 1836. For present work, 2nd ed., Lond. 1841.

The True Principles of Pointed or Christian Architecture, Lond. 1841.

An Apology for the Revival of Christian Architecture in England, Lond. 1843.

The Present State of Ecclesiastical Architecture in England, Lond. 1843.

Glossary of Ecclesiastical Ornament and Costume, Lond. 1844.

Floriated Ornament, Designed by A. Welby Pugin, Lond. 1849.

REDGRAVE, R., 'Importance of the Study of Botany to the Ornamentist', *J. D.*, 1849, I 147—151, 178—185.

'Supplementary Report on Design', *Report by the Juries for the Great Exhibition*, Lond. 1852.

On the Necessity of Principles in Teaching Design, an address, Lond. 1853.

RIGBY, J. S., 'Remarks on Morris' Work', *The Art Workers' Quarterly*, Jan. and Apr. 1902, I 2—5, 61—64.

ROYAL SOCIETY OF ARTS, *A Concise Account of the Rise, Progress, and Present State of the Society for the Encouragement of the Arts, Manufactures, and Commerce, Instituted at London Anno MDCCLIV*. By a Member of the Said Society. Lond. 1763.

RUSKIN, J., *The Collected Works of John Ruskin*, I—XXXIX, Lond. 1903—12.

SEMPER, G., *Wissenschaft, Industrie und Kunst*, Braunschweig 1852.

STANTON, A. P., *Welby Pugin and the Gothic Revival*, unpubl. doctoral thesis, London University, June 1950.

'Some Comments on the Life and Work of Augustus Welby Northmore Pugin', *The Journal of the R.I.B.A.*, Dec. 1952, LX 47—54.

THE STUDIO, *The Art of Christopher Dresser*, Nov. 1898, XV 104—114.

An Interview with Mr. Charles F. Annesley Voysey. Architect and Designer, Sept. 1893, I 231—36.

SUGDEN, V., and EDMONDSON, J. L., *A History of British Wallpaper 1509—1914*, Lond. 1926.

SUMMERSON, J., 'Pugin at Ramsgate', *The Architectural Review*, Apr. 1948, CIII 163—166.

THIIS, J., 'Engelsk Stil og William Morris', *Nordenfjeldske Kunstindustrimuseums Aarbog*, Trondhjem 1900, 179—208.

TOWNDROW, K. R., *Alfred Stevens*, Lond. 1939.

TRAPPES-LOMAX, M., *Pugin*, Sheed and Ward, 1932.

VICTORIA, *Letters of Queen Victoria 1837—1861. A Selection*, Lond. 1907.

VICTORIA AND ALBERT MUSEUM, *Catalogue of an Exhibition in Celebration of the Centenary of William Morris*, Lond. 1934.

Catalogue of an Exhibition of Victorian and Edwardian Decorative Arts, Lond. 1952.

Victorian and Edwardian Decorative Arts, Victoria and Albert Museum Small Picture-book no. 34, Lond. 1952.

VIDALENC, G., *La transformation des arts décoratifs au 19ième siècle: William Morris, son œuvre et son influence*, Caen 1914.

WALLIS, G., *A Letter to the Council of the Manchester School of Design on the System of Instruction Pursued in that School*, signed Oct. 30th, 1845. Lond. 1845.

'Art, Science, and Manufacture as an Unity', *Art Journal*, Oct. 1851, XIII 245—252.

Schools of Art: Their Constitution and Management, Lond. 1857.

British Art, Pictorial, Decorative, and Industrial: A Fifty Years' Retrospect 1832—1882, Lond. and Nottingham 1882.

WATERHOUSE, P., 'The Life and Work of Welby Pugin', *The Architectural Review*, 1897 III 167—175, 211—221, 264—274; 1898, IV 23—27, 67—73, 115 —118, 159—164.

WATT, W., *Hints and Suggestions on Domestic Furniture and Decoration, with a Preface by E. W. Godwin*, Lond. 1877.

WHEWELL, W., *Lectures on the Results of the Great Exhibition of 1851*, 2nd series, Lond. 1853.

WORNUM, R. N., 'Modern Moves in Art', *The Art Journal*, Sept. 1850, XII 269—271.

'The Exhibition as a Lesson in Taste. A Prize Essay', *Art Journ. Exh. Vol.*, Lond. 1851.

'The Governmental Schools of Design', *Art Journal*, Jan. 1852, XIV 16.

WYATT, M. D., *Metal-work and its Artistic Design*, Lond. 1852.

The Industrial Arts of the 19th Century, Lond. 1851—53.

NOTES

CHAPTER I

[1] Notably by Professor Pevsner in *High*.

[2] For this, see Pevsner's analysis, *ibid.*, 67 *seq.*, of Nicolaus Wornum's essay, "The Exhibition as a Lesson in Taste" in *The Art Journal Exhibition Volume*, 1851. Professor Hitchcock, in his book on *Early Victorian Architecture*, also notes, for instance, how "the style of Louis XIV is generally made to include 18th century Rococo" — as in the description, quoted further on, of our *Fig. 4*.

[3] *High*, 36 and 49.

[4] *Geoc*, class XXVI no. 78.

[5] *Ibid.*, Class XXVI no. 202.

[6] 4th Oct. 1851, XIX 433.

[7] Henry Cole, Introduction to *Geoc*, I 31.

[8] Letter to *The Times*, 13th May 1851. *Works*, XII 321.

[9] See *Fig. 15*.

[10] Victoria and Albert Museum, *An Exhibition of Royal Plate*, London, 1954. Catalogue, no. 164.

[11] These six quotations refer to the following exhibits in *Geoc*, Class XXVI: nos. 26, 27, 10, 15, 23, and 55.

[12] *Geoc*, Class XXVI nos. 141, 33, 37a, 48, and 62a.

[13] *The Illustrated London News*, 10th May 1851, XVIII 406, fig. 6.

CHAPTER II

[1] *A Concise Account of the Rise, Progress, and Present State of the Society for the Encouragement of the Arts, Manufactures, and Commerce, Instituted at London Anno MDCCLIV*. By a Member of the Said Society, London, 1763. Title page.

[2] *Ac*, 247.

[3] See Sir Kenneth Clark, *The Gothic Revival*, London, 1950; Michael Trappes-Lomax, *Pugin*, Sheed and Ward, 1932; Ann Phoebe Stanton, *Welby Pugin and the Gothic Revival*, unpublished doctoral thesis, London, 1950.

[4] It is a fact that Barry and Pugin collaborated on the drawings for the competition in 1836; their respective parts in the final result became the subject of heated discussion between their descendants later on. Recent research (Stanton) suggests that the part played by the young Pugin as a "ghost" for Barry, was far more important than has been generally thought, being extended not only to exterior ornament and interior decoration, but even to the elevation and to the general plan. A more moderate standpoint is taken by Hitchcock in his *Early Victorian Architecture*.

[5] Benjamin Ferrey. His *Recollections of A. N. Welby Pugin, and his Father, Augustus Pugin*, London, 1861, has been my basic source of biographical data.

[6] A. P. Stanton, "Some Comments on the Life and Work of Augustus Welby Northmore Pugin", *The Journ. of the R.I.B.A.*, 1952, LX 47—54.

[7] Full title: *Contrasts; or, a Parallel between the noble Edifices of the middle Ages, and corresponding Buildings of the present Day*. I refer to, and quote from, the second edition, of 1841, for greater completeness. For the present purpose, the tendency and basic material are the same in both.

NOTES

8 *Ibid.*, 1 *seq.* and 3, footnote.
9 *Ibid.*, 5 *seq.*
10 *Ibid.*, 7, 8, footnote, and 18.
11 p. 45 *seq.*
12 *Ibid.*, 2—5.
13 *Idem, An Apology for the Revival of Christian Architecture in England*, London, 1843, 21.
14 *Idem, The True Principles*, pp. 11, 1, 42, 1, and 2. — None the less, Pugin had put in a sham plaster ceiling at Alton Towers.
15 *Ibid.*, pp. 30, 35, 30, 56, 55, 58 *seq.*, and 62 *seq.*
16 *The True Principles*, pp. 40, 23, and 24 *seq.* On p. 41 he admits having himself "perpetrated many of these enormities in the furniture I designed some years ago for Windsor Castle [in 1827]. At that time I had not the least idea of the principles I am now explaining; all my knowledge of Pointed Architecture was confined to a tolerably good notion of details in the abstract; but these I employed with so little judgment or propriety, that, although parts were correct and exceedingly well executed, collectively they appeared a complete burlesque of pointed design." Examples of this furniture were shown at the exhibition of *Victorian and Edwardian Design* at The Victoria and Albert Museum, November 1952 — January 1953, and photographs were published in the Exhibition Photographic Catalogue.
17 *Ibid.*, 25 *seq.*
18 *Idem, Floriated Ornament*, London, 1849. Introduction.
19 The last quotation was from Pugin, *The True Principles*, 27.
20 Stanton, *Some Comments*, note 9, adds that Carolani was "a slow worker- a great failing in any assistant to Pugin—and he was in his own right somewhat temperamental".
21 Alphonse-Napoléon Didron, archeologist and painter of stained glass. Best known as founder of *Annales Archéologiques*. The letter is reproduced *in extenso* in my Appendix I.
22 When Pugin published *The Present State of Ecclesiastical Architecture in England*, in 1843, many of his buildings which were then mere projects, and never to be finished, were represented as complete. The whole book is in fact mainly a record of his own work.
23 Ferrey, 259 *seq.*, note 3.
24 *Ibid.*, 250 *seq.*
25 Paul Waterhouse, "The Life and Work of Welby Pugin", *The Architectural Review*, 1897—8, III 264.
26 A. P. Stanton, *Welby Pugin*, 201 and 215.
27 Pugin, *An Apology*, p. 10 and pl. III.

²⁸ *Ibid.* This and the following quotations are from the chapter called "Modern Inventions and Mechanical Improvements", from pp. 38 *seq.* and 22.

²⁹ *Idem, The True Principles,* 67.

³⁰ A. P. Stanton, *Some Comments.*

³¹ Ferrey, 257.

CHAPTER III

Part 1

1 *Report of the Departmental Committee on the Royal College of Art,* London, 1911, 27 *seq.* Quoted from *Ac* 247.

2 See R. C., 1835, V and 1836, IX.

3 *Statutes at Large,* 2 Vic. Chap. XVII. Previously some protection had been afforded by a provisory Act passed in 1787: "An Act for the Encouragement of the Arts of designing and printing Linens, Cottons, Callicoes, and Muslins, by vesting the Properties thereof in the Designers, Printers, and Proprietors, for a limited Time." This was a two-months' patent *(Ibid.* 27 Geo. III. Chap. XXXVIII). This Act was made permanent in 1794 *(Ibid.* 34 Geo. III. Chap. XXIII), and in 1839 extended "to Designs for printing other woven Fabrics" *(Ibid.,* 2 Vic. Chap. XIII).

4 George Wallis, *British Art, Pictorial, Decorative, and Industrial: A Fifty Years' Retrospect, 1832—82. A Lecture,* London, 1882, 12.

5 R. C., 1836, IX 29 *seq.,* 32, and 39.

6 *Ac,* 248.

7 R. C., 1849, XVIII 297 (Digby Wyatt's Report) and *Fifty Years,* I 298.

8 *Ac,* 248.

9 I have not found the word used at an earlier date, and the *N.E.D.* gives no date for its first appearance.

10 For the following information about personal contacts with the Schools of Design, see the respective Reports (R. C., 1849, XVIII); for Henry Cole see also his autobiography *Fifty Years,* I 109 *seq.*

11 Published as a pamphlet by the Department of Science and Art, London, 1854. Also printed, with added comments by the author, in *J. D.,* 1952, VI 1—6.

12 R. C., 1836, IX, Hay's Report.

13 *The Athenaeum,* 1843, 1074—75, 1114—15, 1162—64. The articles are unsigned, but Cole's authorship is warranted through entry in the Victoria and ·Albert Museum Library catalogue.

14 For Cole's biographical data, where no other source is given, I have drawn on *Fifty Years,* I—II. This was unfinished at the death of the author, and was completed and published by his son.

15 *Ibid.,* I, 105.

[16] *Ibid.*, II 178 *seq.*

[17] *Ibid.*, I 107.

[18] The full printed list of those who had "already expressed their willingness to assist in this object", includes "John Absolon. John Bell, Sculptor. C. W. Cope, A.R.A. T. Creswick, A.R.A. J. Herbert, R.A. J. C. Horsley, a Professor of the School of Design. S. Joseph, Sculptor. D. Maclise, R.A. W. Mulready, R.A. R. Redgrave, A.R.A. H. J. Townsend, a Professor of the School of Design. Sir R. Westmacott, R.A. etc. etc." *Advertising Pamphlet for Summerly's Art Manufactures,* London, 1847. Listed in the Bod. Lib., Oxford, under Cole, Sir Henry.

[19] *Ibid.*

[20] Anonymous in *J. D.,* 1850—51, IV 161—64.

[21] The sculptor Alfred Stevens, who designed for H. E. Hoole & Co., of Green Lane Works, Sheffield, Workers in Bronze and Metals. His stoves won the firm a first place at the Great Exhibition. Teacher of architectural drawing, perspective, and modelling at the School of Design 1845—47. *(Dict. of Nat. Biog.,* London, 1909). See also for his work in Sheffield: K. R. Towndrow, *Alfred Stevens,* London, 1939.

[22] In *Fifty Years* (the part of it which was written by Henry Cole's son) he is mentioned as the editor. C. Hobhouse, in *1851 and the Crystal Palace,* follows Cole. N. Pevsner accords the honour to Richard Redgrave, whose "editorship is revealed in a pencilled note at the foot of the preface to the Victoria and Albert Museum copy of Vol. VI *(Matthew Digby Wyatt,* note 10, adjoining p. 38). We may follow Pevsner, but the question is of small significance in the present context.

[23] Preface, 1849, I p. viii.

[24] *J. D.,* 1850, III 87, and 1850—51, IV 75.

[25] *Ibid.,* 1849, I 1—4.

[26] 1849, I 26—29, 64—67, and 91—94.

[27] Pugin, the admirer of Gothic art, had advocated that the *constructive* members in a piece of design should be the most ornate; Dyce, the academic painter trained in a classical atmosphere, wanted to decorate most richly the *relieved* parts. It is interesting to see how their outlook was influenced by their respective backgrounds even on points where they may not themselves have been consciously aware of the true impulse for their reasoning.

[28] *The Two Paths,* lect. 2, 1859. *Works,* XVI 322.

[29] "On the Principles of Design applicable to Textile Art", in *Art Treasures of the U. K. from the Art Treasures Exhibition, Manchester,* London, 1858, II, 77.

[30] "Importance of the Study of Botany to the Ornamentist", *J. D.,* I 147—51 and 178—85.

31 "More upon Shams in Woven Fabrics", *J. D.*, 1850—51, IV 41.

32 1850—51, IV 40.

33 Owen Jones, "Gleanings from the Great Exhibition of 1851", *J. D.*, 1851, V 90 *seq*. In this lecture is also given for the first time the core of those principles later expounded in his lectures of 1852—53, in his *Grammar of Ornament*, 1856, and in *The True and the False in the Decorative Arts*, 1863, where on p. 14 almost identical passages are repeated.

Part 2

34 *High*, 140.

35 Printed in *Report by the Juries on the Subjects in the thirty Classes into which the Exhibition was divided*, London, 1852, 708—49.

36 Reprinted *J. D.*, 1851—52, V 158 *seq*.

37 "An Attempt to define the Principles which should regulate the Employment of Colour, in the decorative Arts." Printed in *Results*, 2nd series, p. 256.

38 Wyatt, "An Attempt to define the Principles which should determine Form in the decorative Arts", *ibid.*, 229 *seq*.

39 "The Exhibiton as a Lesson in Taste", a Prize Essay. *The Art Journal Exhibition Volume*, 1851, p. v.

40 *Loc. cit.*

Part 3

41 "Speech given at the Banquet for Ministers, Foreign Ambassadors, Commissioners of the Exhibition of 1851, and Mayors of the Towns, on March 21st, 1851." *The Principal Speeches and Addresses of His Royal Highness the Prince Consort*, London, 1862, 112.

42 *Fifty Years*, I 297.

43 December 1852. The passage is quoted by Henry Cole in *Fifty Years*, I 285 *seq*.

44 When lecturing at Philadelphia in 1877. *Penn Monthly*, Feb. 1877, p. 119.

45 Letter to Henry Cole, 17th June, 1854. Quoted from K. J. Fielding, "Charles Dickens and the Department of Practical Art", *Mod. Lang. Rev.*, XLVIII 270—77, July 1953. I am indebted for this reference to the late Mr. Humphry House, of Wadham College, Oxford.

46 Charles Dickens, *Hard Times*, The London Edition, The Caxton Publishing Co., London, p. 3 *seq*.

47 See *Fifty Years*, I 283, 305, and 307; II 285.

48 *J.D.*, 1849, I 178.

49 Quoted from *High*, note 30.

50 "The Exhibition as a Lesson in Taste", *The Art Journal Exhibition Volume*, 1851, p. xiv. Ill. p. 132.

51 "Wohin führt die Entwerthung der Materie durch ihre Behandlung mit der Maschine, durch Surrogate für sie und durch so viele neue Erfindungen? Wohin die Entwerthung der Arbeit, der malerischen, bildnerischen oder sonstigen Ausstattung, veranlasst durch die nämlichen Ursachen? Ich meine natürlich nicht ihre Entwerthung im Preise, sondern in der Bedeutung, in der Idee. Ist das neue Parlamentshaus in London nicht durch die Maschine ungeniessbar gemacht worden? Wie wird die Zeit oder die Wissenschaft in diese bis jetzt durchaus verworrenen Zustände Gesetz und Ordnung bringen, wie verhindern, dass sich die allgemeine Entwerthung auch auf das wirklich nach alter Weise von Händen ausgeführte Werk erstrecke, und man anderes nicht darin sehe als Affectation, Alterthümelei, apartes Wesen und Eigensinn?"
Wissenschaft, Industrie und Kunst, Braunschweig, 1852, 19.

52 "ist der Chinese, der mit dem Messer und der Gabel essen soll.... Ich beklage allgemeine Zustände keinesweges, von denen dies nur die weniger wichtigen Symptome sind, sondern bin sicher, dass sie sich früher oder später zum Heile und zur Ehre der Gesellschaft nach allen Seiten glücklich entfalten werden". *Ibid.*, 9 *seq.*

53 "Art, Science, and Manufacture as a Unity", *The Art Journal*, Oct. 1851, 248 *seq.*

54 "On the Facilities afforded to all Classes of the Community for obtaining Education in Art", by Henry Cole, C.B., General Superintendent, and 2. "On the Methods employed for imparting Education in Art to all Classes", by Richard Redgrave, R.A., Art Superintendent. *Addresses of the Superintendents of the Department of Practical Art*, London, 1853.

55 *On the Necessity of Principles in teaching Design*, London, 1853.

56 "Report of the Commissioners on Children's Employment" of 1843, p. 26. Quoted from J. H. Clapham, *An Economic History of Modern Britain. The Early Railway Age*, 1820—50, Cambridge, 1950, 571.

57 "Introductory Address on the Function of the Science and Art Department." Extracts printed in *Fifty Years*, II 289.

58 *Ac*, 256.

59 *Suggestions towards the Stimulation of a national Feeling for Art at the Close of the London Exhibition of Industry.*

60 April 21st. Printed in *Results*, 1853.

61 Not all of them written by Jones himself: J. B. Waring wrote on Byzantine and Elizabethan Ornament, J. O. Westwood on Celtic, and M. D. Wyatt on Renaissance and on the "Italian Periods".

[62] *Grammar of Ornament,* Introduction. These Principles had been elaborated probably in roughly the same form in some lectures delivered by Owen Jones at Marlborough House in June, 1852; but these lectures were published only in 1863, under the title of *The True and the False in the Decorative Arts.* Here Jones quoted as authorities for his own principles passages from Pugin, Ruskin, Wyatt, Seroux d'Agincourt, Sir Charles Eastlake, Redgrave, Fergusson, and Vitruvius. As for colour, he derived his "invaluable rules from the works of Mr. Field." *(The True and the False,* 56).

[63] "The Exhibition as a Lesson in Taste", *The Art Journal Exhibition Volume,* 1851, p. i.

[64] In *The True and the False.* No authorities are quoted in the *Grammar.*

[65] Warranted by the text accompanying the Moorish plates, pp. 66—72.

[66] Warranted by text on p. 79.

[67] "Victorian Progress in Applied Design", *The Art Journal Royal Jubilee Number,* 1887, 187 *seq.*

[68] *Op. cit.,* 155 *seq*

[69] *Metal-Work and its artistic Design,* London, 1852, p. xi.

[70] *Results,* 227.

[71] "individuellen Ausdruck, die Sprache, die phonetische höhere Schöne, die Seele, ... sobald der Gegenstand nicht bloss sich selbst Zweck ist, sondern irgend eine Nutzbarkeit, eine Bestimmung hat. Tritonen, Nereiden und Nymphen werden immer an einem Brunnen Bedeutung erhalten, Venus und die Grazien an einem Spiegel, Trophäen und Kämpfe an Waffen." *Wissenschaft, Industrie und Kunst,* 25.

[72] "Supplementary Report on Design", *Report of the Juries,* 722 *seq.*

[73] *Grammar of Ornament,* 156.

[74] *J. D.,* 1850—51, IV 12 *seq.*

CHAPTER IV

[1] For Ruskin's relations with Pugin, see Trappes-Lomax, *Pugin,* London, 1932, 313—28. Ruskin was generally thought to have borrowed freely from Pugin's writings, a charge which he denied — and as it seems, with justice. For his own opinion on Pugin's work, see his "Romanist Modern Art", *Works,* IX 436—440. — An explanation of their similar attitude on many points, however, should also be sought in the general intellectual atmosphere of the time. As for Ruskin, it no longer seems justifiable to consider him the one and only original exponent, in his day, of certain trends of thought which, more or less distinctly expressed, were in the air. His views, in the *Seven Lamps* and elsewhere, correspond on many points to what had been and was still being expounded by members of church-reforming bodies like

The Camden Society and *The Ecclesiological Society*, and was expressed in contributions to *The Ecclesiologist*. In his preference for earlier forms of Gothic, Ruskin also seems to follow a general trend of the day. For a more thorough study of early Victorian architecture and the ideas which motivated its form, I must refer my readers to the excellent and thorough research made by Henry-Russel Hitchcock. (See book-list.)

2 *SV*, II ch. vi § 71 and 69. *Works*, X 239 and 237.

3 There is a quotation from Wordsworth on the title page of the first volume of *Modern Painters*, where Ruskin's ideas of a divinely inspired Nature are set forth for the first time.

4 *MP*, II ch. iii § 10. *Works*, IV 59.

5 *MP*, I ch. vi § 5. *Works*, III 111.

6 *The Two Paths*, lect. I § 14. *Works*, XVI 268.

7 *SL*, Lamp of Beauty § 3. *Works*, VIII 141.

8 *Ibid.*, Lamp of Truth § 9—10. *Works*, VIII 66, 67.

9 *SV*, I Appendix xvii. *Works*, IX 455 *seq.*

10 *The Two Paths*, lecture IV. *Works*, XVI 349.

11 This and the following quotations have all been taken from *SV*, II ch. vi, "On the Nature of Gothic".

12 *Fors Clavigera*, Letter 79 § 8, July 1877. *Works*, XXIX 154.

13 *SV*, II ch. vi § 17. *Works*, X 196—7.

14 *Lectures on Art*, lect. IV § 123. *Works*, XX 113.

15 *The Two Paths*, lect. III § 92. *Works*, XVI 341.

16 *Lectures on Art*, lect. IV § 116. *Works*, XX 107.

17 *SV*, II ch. vi § 21. *Works*, X 201.

18 *A Joy for Ever*, lect. I § 28. *Works*, XVI 34.

19 *The Two Paths*, lect. III § 71. *Works*, XVI 319.

20 Quoted in Editors' Introduction to *Works*, XVI xxix.

21 *Munera Pulveris*, ch. V § 108. *Works*, XVII 233.

22 *Lectures on Art*, lect. IV § 123. *Works*, XX 113.

23 *Modern Art*, a Lecture. *Works*, XIX 214.

24 *SV*, I ch. xx § 16. *Works*, IX 264.

25 This was used as a subtitle to *Laws of Fésole*. *Works*, XV 351.

26 *SL*, Introductory. *Works*, VIII 20—21.

27 *Ibid.*, Lamp of Beauty §§ 3 and 15. *Works*, VIII 142, 154.

28 *SV*, I ch. xx § 17. *Works*, IX 265 *seq.*

29 *Ibid.*, Appendix XVII. *Works*, IX 456.

30 *SL*, Lamp of Truth § 20. *Works*, VIII 84.

31 *SV*, I Appendix XVII. *Works*, IX 456.

32 *Works*, XVI 427—430 Appendix I. Ruskin's own remarks quoted from *Journal of the Society of Arts*, March 14, 1856, LV 298—99.

33 Letter to Dr. Ackland, on the Oxford Museum, 20th Jan. 1859. *Works*, XVI 232.

34 *The Two Paths*, Lect. III § 73—76, and Lect. I § 47. *Works*, XVI 320 *seq.* and 288.

35 *The Study of Architecture*, a lecture. *Works*, XIX 38.

1 Preface to Ruskin's "On the Nature of Gothic", from *SV*, as printed by the Kelmscott Press in 1892. *MM*, I 292.

2 "How I became a Socialist" (1894). *Works*, XXIII 279.

3 "The Lesser Arts of Life" (1877). *Works*, XXII 239.

4 "The Prospects of Architecture" (1881). *Ibid.*, 143.

5 "The Revival of Handicraft" (1888). *Ibid.*, 336.

6 "How we live and how we might live" (1885). *Works*, XXIII 24.

7 "The Revival of Handicraft" (1888). *Works*, XXII 335 *seq.*

8 "Some Hints on Pattern-designing" (1881). *Ibid.*, 203 *seq.*

9 "The Society of the Future" (1888). *MM*, II 458.

10 Only in the matter of sex does he seem to have been frustrated; it is questionable whether his marriage was happy in the sense that it gave him the satisfaction of intimate mental and physical contact with his beautiful and silent wife. Some critics have assigned his recurrent periods of gloom to this particular cause (*vide* Philip Henderson, *The Letters of William Morris*, Introduction). In view of Morris's several emphatic denunciations of contemporary sexual conventions, there is a certain amount to be said for such a view.

11 "The Society of the Future" (1888). *MM*, II 457.

12 *Ibid.*, 456.

13 "Socialism and Anarchism" (1889). *Ibid.*, 313.

14 Quoted from Morris by May Morris. *Ibid.*, 316

15 "At a Picture-show" (1884). *Ibid.*, 412.

16 "The Prospects of Architecture" (1881). *Works*, XXII 149.

17 *News from Nowhere* (1890). *Works*, XVI 43.

18 "Art and the Beauty of the Earth" (1881). *Works*, XXII 163.

19 "Art and Industry in the 14th Century" (1890). *Ibid.*, 388.

20 "The Lesser Arts" (1877). *Ibid.*, 3.

21 "At a Picture-show" (1884). *MM*, II 414.

22 The same year in which he was appointed Examiner of drawings sent in for competition at the South Kensington School of Art, working in this capacity together with Lewis F. Day, the designer and author of books on design. It should be noted that Morris's contact with the officials of the Victoria and Albert Museum was very close; his advice was sought

particularly on Eastern textile art, on manuscripts, and on early printed books; on several occasions he acted as the instrument for valuable acquisitions.

[23] Titles of lectures delivered respectively in 1880 and 1881. *Works*, XXII 51 and 155.

[24] For an extensive account of major dated works of the Firm, *vide* G. Vidalenc, *La transformation des arts décoratifs*, Caen, 1914 Appendix I. Also *Mac*.

[25] *Mac*, II 39.

[26] Ill. in S. Tschudi Madsen, "Viktoriansk dekorativ Kunst", *Nordenfjeldske Kunstindustrimuseums Årbok*, Trondheim, 1952.

[27] *Exh*, 38.

[28] *Exh*, I 6, p. 41.

[29] "Making the Best of it" (about 1879). *Works*, XXII 106.

[30] "Some Hints on Pattern-designing" (1881). *Ibid.*, 177.

[31] "Making the Best of it" (1879). *Ibid.*, 105.

[32] "Some Hints on Pattern-designing". *Ibid.*, 195 *seq.*

[33] "Gothic Architecture" (1889). *MM*, I 266.

[34] "The Lesser Arts" (1877). *Works*, XXII 15.

[35] "The Society of the Future" (1888). *MM*, II 454.

[36] "The English Preraphaelites" (1891). *MM*, I 303.

[37] "Art and the Beauty of the Earth" (1881). *Works*, XXII 155, 167 *seq.*, and 155.

[38] "Making the Best of it" (1879). *Ibid.*, 114 *seq.*

[39] "The Art of the People" (1879). *Ibid.*, 47.

[40] "The Lesser Arts" (1877). *Ibid.*, 20.

[41] "Some Hints on Pattern-designing" (1881). *Ibid.*, 186.

[42] This and the following quotations have been taken from "Making the Best of it" (1879). *Works*, XXII 103 *seq.*

[43] "Art and the Beauty of the Earth" (1881). *Ibid.*, 169.

[44] These and the following quotations have been taken from "Some Hints on Pattern-designing". *Ibid.*, 190 *seq.*

[45] "An Address to Students at Birmingham" (1894). *Ibid.*, 436.

[46] "Making the Best of it" (1879). *Ibid.*, 100 and 109 *seq.*

[47] "Some Hints on Pattern-designing" (1881). *Ibid.*, 199.

[48] *Exh*, I 24, p. 45.

[49] "Making the Best of it" (1879). *Works*, XXII 110.

[50] "The lesser Arts" (1877). *Works*, XXII 261 *seq.*

[51] "Making the Best of it" (1879). *Works*, XXII 113.

[52] "The Beauty of Life" (1880). *Works*, XXII 77.

1 For information about him, I have drawn mainly on D. Harbron, *The Conscious Stone; the Life of Edward William Godwin*, London, 1949.

2 *Ibid.*, 32 seq.

3 Ill. in *Victoria and Albert Museum Small Picture-book no. 34*, London, 1952.

4 See for ill. W. Watt, *Hints and Suggestions on Domestic Furniture*, London, 1877.

5 An article in *The Architect*, Aug. 1875, quoted by Harbron in *The Conscious Stone*, 78.

6 E. W. Godwin, *Dress*, London, 1884, 1.

7 I seem to remember having seen a small table in ebonised wood, of a typical Godwin design, in Morris's house at Kelmscott when I last visited it in April 1953. The table was then placed in a room on the ground floor, close to the stairs leading to the first floor.

8 Preface, vii.

9 *Idem*, "The Fashion of Furniture", *The Cornhill Magazine*, March 1864, IX 349.

10 Peter Floud, having examined "several thousand actual samples of wall-papers, textiles, and carpets, dating from 1850 to 1860", found that "as far as wallpapers and carpets are concerned, a real revolution in design had already occurred before Morris founded his firm in 1861". When compared to the formal programme of the "reformers", he also considers Morris's designs to be traditional in their expression, and conservative of mid-Victorian tendencies. *Vide The Listener*, October 7th and 14th 1954.

11 I have found several references in the writings of William Morris to the early activities of the Department of Practical Art. They are on the whole very appreciative, and show that Morris himself must have possessed a thorough knowledge of them.

12 By Nikolaus Pevsner, in *Pioneers of the Modern Movement from William Morris to Walter Gropius*, London, 1936.

13 Lewis F. Day, "Victorian Progress in Applied Design", *The Art Journal Royal Jubilee Number*, June 1887, N. S. VII 185—202.

14 Preface, p. 3. The plate is no. 8 of the 20th Chapter.

15 They were *Unity in Variety* and *The Rudiments of Botany* in 1859, and *A Popular Manual of Botany* in 1860.

16 I am indebted for this information to Mr. John Lowry of the Victoria and Albert Museum Circulation Department, who had it from Dresser's daughter, Miss Nelly Dresser.

17 *Exh*, 35.

18 Obituary note in *The Builder*, 1904, LXXXVII 610.

[19] "The Art of Christopher Dresser", *The Studio*, 1898, XV 104 *seq.*

[20] "Christopher Dresser, Industrial Designer", *The Arch. Rev.*, 1937, LXXXI 184. Pevsner's figures are based on studies of Dresser's notebooks shown to him before the last War by his daughters, but later destroyed.

[21] *The Studio, loc. cit.*

[22] Report from the opening, *The British Architect*, 1879, XII 4.

[23] *A. D.*, 2.

[24] *Studies in Design*, 8.

[25] *P. D.*, 75.

[26] Jones's fifth Proposition, Appendix I.

[27] *P. D.*, 138.

[28] *A. D.*, 1.

[29] *P. D.*, 64 and 69.

[30] *A. D.*, 50, 70, 72, and 83.

[31] *Ibid.*, 6.

[32] *Ibid.*, 168 and 171 *seq.*, pl. XVI.

[33] This cabinet was shown in the exhibition "Um 1900, Art Nouveau und Jugendstil", held at the Kunstgewerbemuseum, Zürich, 28 June to 28 Sept., 1952. Objects were given no numbers or descriptions in the *Wegleitung 194 des Kunstgewerbemuseums Zürich*, which was published for the occasion.

[34] *P. D.*, 17, ill. fig. 12, on p. 18.

[35] *Idem, Studies in Design*, Pl. III, and accompanying text.

[36] *P. D.*, 22 *seq.*, and 16 *seq.*

[37] *Ibid.*, 33, 140, and 50 *seq.* It was according to this last principle that he had criticised, very severely, some of the exhibits of the then little known firm of Morris & Co., writing with horror of what was, "as the label informs us, 'Two stained and gilded DRAWING-ROOM chairs!!'"—It was probably his sense of economy as well as of practical utility which forbade him to "commend these as works of beauty". The Morris embroideries, however, he praised as being "simple, quaint, and pleasing", finding that "the parts are well made out and the pattern is telling.... while the effect is quaint, simple, and good". (Christopher Dresser, *Development of Ornamental Art in the International Exhibition*, London, 1862, 85 and 106.) This is the only example I know of either Morris or Dresser speaking or writing one about the other.

[38] *P. D.*, 16, 120, and 157.

[39] *Ibid.*, 126.

[40] I am indebted for this information to Mr. Hugh Wakefield of the Victoria and Albert Museum Circulation Dept., London.

[41] Described in *Exh*, 35, no. H 20.

[42] In *P. D.*

LIST OF ILLUSTRATIONS

Fig. 1. *The Great Exhibition Official Descriptive and Illustrated Catalogue*, I, sect. ii, class 10, no. 96.

Fig. 2. *Ibid.*, I, sect. ii, class 10, no. 427.

Fig. 3. *Ibid.*, I, sect. ii, class 10, no. 496.

Fig. 4. *Ibid.*, II, sect. iii, class 26, no. 183.

Fig. 5. *Ibid.*, II, sect. iii, class 22, no. 244.

Fig. 6. *Ibid.*, II, sect. iii, class 22, no. 373.

Fig. 7. *The Illustrated London News*, May 10th 1851, XVIII 402, fig. 16.

Fig. 8. PUGIN, A. W. N., *Contrasts*, London, 1836, plate not numbered: 'Contrasted Episcopal Residences': Ely House, Dover Street, 1836, Ely Palace, Holborn, 1536.

Fig. 9. *Idem, The True Principles of Pointed or Christian Architecture*, London, 1841, 41, 'Illustration of the Extravagant Style of Modern Gothic Furniture and Decoration'.

Fig. 10. *Idem, Floriated Ornament*, London, 1849, pl. 16, conventionalised ornaments of
(1) Rosa Englenteria,
(2) Rosa Muscata Alba,
(3) Libanotis,
(4) Cistus Ledon Myrtiforium,
(5) Herba Benedicta.

Fig. 11. *Idem, An Apology for the Revival of Christian Architecture*, London, 1843, pl. III.
To the left: 'Railway Bridges on the Antient Principles',
To the right: 'A Show Front with Convenient Additions'.

Fig. 12. Tea-pot and cup with saucer, earthenware, made by Minton and Co., Staffordshire, 1846, under the supervision of Henry Cole. Given a prize at the Exhibition of the Society of Arts 1846. In the Victoria and Albert Museum.
Vide H. COLE, *Fifty Years*, II 178 and *Exh* A 7 and A 8, p. 9 *seq.*

Fig. 13. REDRAVE, R., 'Supplementary Report on Design', *Report by the Juries for the Great Exhibition*, London, 1852, 722.
Listed in *Geoc*, France no. 1231.

Fig. 14. *J. D.*, 1850—51, IV 13, 'Shop Front of Mr. Chappell's the Music-seller, in New Bond Street, designed by Owen Jones, manufactured by Burnett, of Deptford'.

Fig. 15. Capital from the Oxford Museum, in the great glass-roofed court: No. 2 to left from main entrance, column 5.

177

Fig. 16. Cabinet, designed by Philip Webb, 1861, front painted by William Morris with scenes from the legend of St. George. Exh. in the Green Dining-room, Victoria and Albert Museum, London. *Exh*, I 5, p. 41.

Fig. 17. Design for 'Blackthorn' wallpaper, by William Morris, 1892. *Exh*, I 76, p. 49.

Fig. 18. Embroidered wall-hanging, wool on linen. Designed by William Morris about 1880 and probably worked by Margaret Bell (wife of Sir Lowthian Bell). Exh. in the Green Dining-room, Victoria and Albert Museum, London. *Exh*, I 24, p. 45.

Fig. 19. Escritoire and stand, marquetry of sycamore and various woods. Designed by George Jack, 1893. Made by Morris and Co. *Exh*, I 15, p. 42.

Fig. 20. Coffee table, ebonised wood, made in numbers by William Watt, and Collinson and Lock, from about 1868. Originally owned by Ellen Terry. W. Watt pl. 15. *Exh*, K 4, p. 57.

Fig. 21. DRESSER, CHRISTOPHER, *The Art of Decorative Design*, London, 1862, pl. XII.

Fig. 22. *Idem, P.D.*, London, Paris, and New York, 1873, Fig. 12. Full text and explanation in note p. 17: 'I have given in this chapter an original sketch (Fig. 12), in which I have sought to embody chiefly the one idea of power, energy, force, or vigour; and in order to do this, I have employed such lines as we see in the bursting buds of spring, when the energy of growth is at its maximum, and especially such as are to be seen in the spring growth of a luxuriant tropical vegetation; I have also availed myself of those forms to be seen in certain bones of birds which are associated with the organs of flight, and which give us an impression of great strength, as well as those observable in the powerful propelling fins of certain species of fish.'

Fig. 23. *Idem, Studies in Design*, London, Paris, and New York, 1876, pl. III.

Fig. 24. *Idem, P.D.*, Figs. 31 and 32.

Fig. 25. Glass designed by Christopher Dresser, executed by J. Cooper and Sons, producers of *Clutha* glass.
Vide 'The Art of Christopher Dresser', *The Studio*, 1898, XV 104—14.

Fig. 26. Tea-pot, electro-plate with ebony handle. Stamped '*Chr. Dresser*' (facsimile signature). Made by James Dickson and Son about 1880. Owned by the makers. *Exh*, H 20, p. 35.

I am indebted for the illustrations to:
The Bodleian Library, Oxford *(Figs.* 1—7)
The City Gallery, Bristol *(Fig.* 20)
The Editor of *The Studio (Fig.* 25)

The Victoria and Albert Museum, Crown Copyright *(Figs.* 8—14, 16—19, and 21—24)

Mr. S. Constantine, Director of the firm James Dixon & Sons, Ltd., Sheffield *(Fig.* 26)

Mr. Donald Whitton, Fellow of Lincoln College, Oxford *(Fig.* 15).

It has proved impossible to obtain an answer to a series of letters to the Museum of Arts and Crafts *(Kunstgewerbemuseum)* in Zürich. Because of this I am, to my great regret, unable to reproduce any objects from their interesting exhibition *Jugend—Art Nouveau,* which I visited in 1952.

LIST OF ABBREVIATIONS

COLE, Sir Henry : *Fifty Years of Public Work*, I–II,
London, 1884 = *Fifty Years*

DRESSER, Chris. : *The Art of Decorative Design*, London, 1862 = *A. D.*

—»— : *Principles of Decorative Design*, London, 1873 = *P. D.*

*The Great Exhibition, Official Descriptive and Illustrated
Catalogue, I—III*, London, 1851 = *Geoc*

The Journal of Design and Manufacture,
London, 1849–1852 = *J. D.*

MACKAIL, J. W. : *The Life of William Morris*, I–II,
London, 1899. ed. O.U.P., World's
Classics, 1950 = *Mac*

MORRIS, May : *William Morris, Artist, Writer, Socialist, I–II*, Oxford, 1936 = *MM*

MORRIS, William : *The Collected Works of William
Morris*, I–XXIV, London, 1910–15 = *Works*

The New English Dictionary = *N. E. D.*

PEVSNER, Nikolaus: *Academies of Art, Past and Present*,
Cambridge, 1940 = *Ac*

—»— : *High Victorian Design*, London, 1951 = *High*

Reports from Committees = R.C.

RUSKIN, John : *The Collected Works of John Ruskin*,
I—XXXIX, London, 1903–12 = *Works*

—»— : *Modern Painters*, I—V, London, 1843
—60, *Works*, III—VII = *MP*

—»— : *The Seven Lamps of Architecture*,
London, 1849, *Works*, VIII = *SL*

—»— : *The Stones of Venice*, I–III, London,
1851–53, *Works*, IX—XI = *SV*

*Victoria & Albert Museum, Catalogue of an Exhibi-
tion of Victorian & Edwardian Decorative Arts*, London, 1952 = *Exh*

WHEWELL, W. : *Lectures on the Results of the Great
Exhibition of 1851*, 2nd series, Lon-
don, 1853. = *Results*